# Trail to Disaster

By Patricia Joy Richmond

With a Foreword by Mary Lee Spence

**Trail to Disaster**
The Route of
John C. Frémont's Fourth
Expedition from Big Timbers,
Colorado, through the San
Luis Valley, to Taos,
New Mexico

COLORADO
HISTORICAL
SOCIETY

University Press of Colorado

Published by the University Press of Colorado
P.O. Box 849
Niwot, Colorado 80544

The University Press of Colorado is a cooperative publishing enterprise supported, in part, by Adams State College, Colorado State University, Fort Lewis College, Mesa State College, Metropolitan State College of Denver, University of Colorado, University of Northern Colorado, University of Southern Colorado, and Western State College.

ISBN: 0-87081-275-0

The paper used in this publication meets the minimum requirements of the American National Standard for Information Sciences—Permanence of Paper for Printed Library Materials. ANSI Z39.48–1984

∞

10  9  8  7  6  5  4  3  2  1

Cover: Scratchboard painting of Christmas Camp, by Charles Ewing. Courtesy of the Rio Grande County Museum, Inc.

# CONTENTS

## Illustrations

## Maps

# Foreword

BY MARY LEE SPENCE
University of Illinois, Urbana-Champaign

IN THIS LITTLE VOLUME, Patricia Richmond traces with great detail and accuracy the route of one of John C. Frémont's most painful expeditions. In addition to a careful combing of available documents and maps, historical and modern, she has made numerous trips into the disaster area over many years and in all seasons and in all kinds of weather. Familiarity with the San Luis Valley and the San Juan Mountains permits her to write not only with authority, but graphically, and the reader is swept up in the agony of men as they battle the mountains and the winter--and lose.

Although designed to ascertain the practicality, in winter, of a transcontinental railroad route along the 38th parallel, the expedition was not being sponsored by the United States government, but by private individuals, and perhaps even by Frémont and his father-in-law, the influential Senator Thomas Hart Benton of Missouri. In spite of its unofficial character, the men who went with Frémont must have had every confidence in their famous leader, who brought considerable talent and experience in exploration to this 1848-49 adventure.

John Charles Frémont had been born on January 21, 1813, in Savannah, Georgia, to Charles Fremon, a French émigré, and to Ann Beverly Whiting, who had scandalized Richmond, Virginia, by leaving her elderly husband, John Pryor, to run away with her lover. Although Pryor petitioned the Virginia legislature for a divorce, there is no evidence that it was ever granted before Fremon's death in 1818. To the "knowing," Frémont grew up with the stigma of illegitimacy and in a family with unstable finances. It is not clear when the *t* was added to the name, but young Frémont began using the accented form when he became associated with Joseph N. Nicollet. After the death of the father, the mother took the family, which now included a second son and a daughter, to live in Charleston, South Carolina. John was prepared for the College of Charleston where he was enrolled in 1829 as a junior in the Scientific Department, but was dismissed in 1831, three months short of graduation, for "incorrigible negligence."

Through the influence of Joel Poinsett, South Carolinian and former minister to Mexico, he obtained in 1833 a civilian post as a teacher of mathematics to midshipmen on board the U.S.S. *Natchez*; 1836-37 found him assisting in the surveys of the projected Charleston and Cincinnati Railroad and the Cherokee country. The great opportunity for his career came in 1838, when, again due to the influence of Poinsett, who was then secretary of war, he was commissioned a second lieutenant in the United States Corps of Topographical Engineers and assigned to accompany the French scientist Nicollet on a reconnaissance of the Minnesota country. The two-year expedition with Nicollet and the subsequent labors in Washington on the report and map of the survey "proved to be Frémont's 'Yale College and his Harvard'" as William Goetzmann has noted. By working with the French scientist, Frémont learned sophisticated methods of geodetic surveying, including using the barometer to measure altitude, a considerable amount of geology, how to manage an expedition, and care in taking astronomical observations. No doubt his mentor encouraged him to read the works of the world-renowned geographer Alexander von Humboldt, and his knowledge of plants must have been enriched through contact with Charles Geyer, the botanist for Nicollet's foray and later for Frémont's 1841 survey of the Raccoon Fork of the Des Moines River.

It was in Washington that he met Jessie, the vivacious daughter of Senator Benton. The two eloped on October 19, 1841, when the bride was but seventeen, but the alliance was to prove extremely valuable to the advancement of Frémont's career.

By the spring of 1842 he was deemed ready for his own command and was ordered to survey the Platte River "up to the head of the Sweetwater." Taking along twenty-one *voyageurs*, principally Creole and Canadian; the skilled German cartographer Charles Preuss; Lucien B. Maxwell as hunter; Kit Carson as guide; and such interesting items as a daguerreotype camera and an india rubber boat, Frémont reached South Pass and then struck northwest to reconnoiter the Wind River Mountains and to scale Woodrow Wilson, one of the highest peaks in the chain. The next year he was ordered to connect this survey with the surveys that naval commander Charles Wilkes had made of the Pacific Coast. When Frémont returned to St. Louis some fourteen months later, he had made a virtual circuit of the entire West. Not only had he examined the northeastern extremity of the Great Salt Lake and visited Fort Vancouver, but he had also effected a rash midwinter crossing of the Sierra Nevada in the vicinity of Carson Pass. His starving men recouped and refitted at Sutter's Fort on the Sacramento, and then traveling south through California with the Sierra on their left, they went through Oak Creek Pass, picked up the Old Spanish Trail and kept to it until the desire to make a cursory examination of Utah Lake forced a departure. After penetrating the Wasatch and Uinta Mountains, Frémont headed for Bent's Fort on the Arkansas, traversing the three parks of the Rockies en route.

With the help of his talented wife, he wrote lively, readable reports of these two expeditions and with the assistance of Preuss drew maps which changed the entire picture of the West. The maps and reports were ordered published by Congress, and subsequently a number of commercial editions appeared at home and abroad. He became a national hero, was breveted captain, and then while he was away on his third expedition (1845-47), which took him into California again, was commissioned a lieutenant colonel in the Mounted Rifles.

In eight short years he had advanced from an unknown second lieutenant to one of the most admired and talked-of lieutenant colonels in the army. His wife jubilantly wrote to him that he was ranked with Daniel Defoe. "They say that as *Robinson Crusoe* is the most natural and interesting fiction of travel, so Frémont's report is the most romantically truthful."

During the third expedition, Frémont became involved with the Americans in their Bear Flag Rebellion against Mexico. His battalion of volunteers, composed of *voyageurs* from his topographical party and American settlers in California, became known as the California Battalion and served under the command of Robert F. Stockton, who became chief of naval and land operations on the Pacific Coast and who later appointed Frémont governor of the conquered territory. The arrival in California of Brigadier General Stephen Watts Kearny, however, created problems for Frémont. He became caught in the middle in the ensuing struggle between Kearny and Stockton for supremacy of command. He chose the wrong side, was ordered to march east behind Kearny's army and, in spite of his father-in-law's efforts, was ultimately court-martialed and convicted on charges of mutiny, disobedience, and conduct prejudiced to military discipline. President James K. Polk remitted the penalty and ordered him to duty again, but Frémont, unwilling to admit in any way the justice of the decision, resigned from the army, and he and Jessie began making plans to settle in California.

Jessie would go west by sea and the Isthmus of Panama, but John, clinging to his career as an explorer, planned a land expedition to gather additional geographical and scientific information. When Benton failed to obtain financing from Congress for Frémont for further surveys, St. Louis businessmen offered contributions, and some veterans of his former expeditions volunteered to go out with him and even recruited others who wished to see what California offered in the way of a future. Richard Kern, the artist, cavalierly explained to a friend that the trip across the continent was "an opportunity to improve myself [in] landscape painting."

The expedition came to be composed largely of gentlemen and artisans, rather than of artisans, trappers, and *voyageurs* as had been true of the three previous expeditions. Many were independent spirits; some were paying their own way, perhaps even supplying their own equipment. The men did not take orders easily, and perhaps they resented the fact that on the trail they were sometimes expected to do the work of muleteers. Furthermore, quite a few were greenhorns and some were very young and inexperienced in the survival techniques of the West. These factors no doubt contributed to disaster. But not to be ignored, either, were the unusually cold winter with its knife-sharp winds and waist-deep snow and the mood of the leader. At this particular time he was a brooding, proud man who needed to win new laurels in exploration in order to wipe out the humiliation of the court-martial.

After the emaciated survivors straggled into Taos, Frémont refitted part of his men and pushed on to California, going down the Rio Grande and then westward along the Gila route to Los Angeles. From there he went to his 44,000-acre Mariposa estate, located not far from Yosemite Valley, which had been purchased for him in 1847 by Thomas O. Larkin. It proved to have rich gold-bearing veins, and for the next few years he was occupied with raising capital for the development of the gold mines and with litigation over the title to the estate, which he finally received in February 1856. But the mercurial explorer had little business acumen, and he lost control of the property in 1864.

In the meantime, however, he had briefly served California in the United States Senate and had made a fifth expedition into the West. As had been true for the fourth, this 1853-54 expedition, also seeking a railroad route, passed through southern Colorado and the San Luis Valley. It endured several weeks of hardship crossing the Great Basin of Utah before traversing the Sierra Nevada below the 36th parallel, probably at Bird Spring Pass or Walker's southern pass.

Because of his popularity with the masses and the fact

that he was not identified with the bitter conflict between the Whigs and the Free-Soilers, Frémont was nominated in 1856 for president by the newly formed Republican Party. The reading public devoured the details of buffalo hunts, night vigils, and blizzards in various campaign biographies, and thousands marched to the slogan Free Speech, Free Men, and Frémont. He did extremely well, garnering 33 percent of the popular vote (45 percent in the North). Had he been successful in Pennsylvania and either Illinois or Indiana, he would have won the election. He took his defeat philosophically, although it must have been a bitter pill to lose the four electoral votes of California where numerous "Bear Clubs" had been organized to support him.

When the Civil War began, President Abraham Lincoln made Frémont a major general and put him in command of the Western Department with headquarters at St. Louis. In this command he lasted approximately one hundred days. Missouri was divided in its loyalties; arms and supplies were insufficient; unscrupulous speculators--some his own California friends--surrounded him; and criticism and military defeats cost him Lincoln's confidence. The president removed him after the general refused to rescind his famous proclamation freeing the slaves of disloyal slaveowners of Missouri, which had been wildly popular with Harriet Beecher Stowe and other antislavery people. Later he held a brief command in western Virginia and was nominated again for the presidency in 1864 by the radical wing of the Republican party, but withdrew before the election.

He now bought a fine home--Pocaho--on the Hudson River and turned his attention to making money, primarily in railroad promotion. The circumstances surrounding the bankruptcy of the Memphis and El Paso in 1870 blemished his reputation and left him virtually penniless. His wife turned to writing to bring in some income, and not until his friend Rutherford B. Hayes was inaugurated president was Frémont able to acquire a federal post. He became territorial governor of Arizona in 1878 and hoped to recoup his finances in mine promotion and speculation and in various land and railroad schemes, some even across the Mexican border. Long absences from the territory brought criticism, and President Arthur asked for his resignation, which he submitted on October 11, 1881.

A second fortune was never made. Even his *Memoirs*, published in 1887, did not bring the expected royalties. With their spinster daughter, Lily, the Frémonts moved to California. Their two sons, John Charles, Jr., and Frank Preston, were elsewhere serving as officers in the navy and army, respectively. From Los Angeles, Frémont occasionally traveled to New York by railroad and was there when he died on July 13, 1890, a few months after Congress had authorized the president to appoint him a major general in the army and to place him on the retired list for pension purposes.

In physical appearance Frémont was about 5 feet 10 inches, slender, upright with finely chiseled features. In 1845, when he was about to embark on the third expedition, artist Alfred S. Waugh found him "a pale intellectual looking young man, modest and unassuming, seemingly more accustomed to the refinements and luxuries of life than to the toils and dangers of the wilderness." His voice was "low and musical," his manners "bland and gentlemanly." After the 1848-49 ordeal, Bayard Taylor remarked that he had "seen in no other man the qualities of lightness, activity, strength, and physical endurance in so perfect an equilibrium." A member of his staff during the Civil War remembered that "he had an eye like a falcon for keenness and earnestness, but tinkling with merriment on slight provocation." He had never heard him use a profane or vulgar expression or known him to drink any intoxicant beyond a glass of claret with his dinner.

Frémont's proudest achievements came before he was forty--exploring the West and making it known to a nation hungry to know. He did more than any previous explorer to point the way west, and so popular was he that eventually twelve towns--east and west of the Mississippi--and countless city streets and schools would bear the name of Frémont. Throughout the early twentieth century, legends of Frémont's daring adventures with his friend Kit Carson would continue to excite the imaginations of young and old as America moved from an era of discovery and exploration toward an age of invention and material progress. Today, books, magazines, and television allow many who will never climb a mountain or wander much farther than a local shopping center to continue to share the moments of excitement that marked the life of John Charles Frémont, America's Pathmarker.

A S A GRADUATE STUDENT attending Adams State College in Alamosa, Colorado, I received an assignment to write a short paper about western history using primary sources. A few weeks earlier a small party from Del Norte, Colorado, had visited the area of John Charles Frémont's Christmas Camp in the San Juan Mountains. My work with the San Luis Valley Historical Society made me aware that diaries and letters of members of the fourth expedition were available. The paper was written quickly. While awaiting the end of the grading period, however, I often would awaken at 2:00 A.M. with a nagging feeling that something was wrong. In the morning I would reread my work and satisfy myself that punctuation, spelling, grammar, and usage were correct.

The night before the paper was due, I sat up in my bed at 2:00 A.M. and announced out loud, "The mileages are wrong!" Following the lead of contemporary historians in routing Frémont to the Rio Grande, I had ignored diary entries describing a two-day ordeal to reach the north end of the sand dunes. The rest of the night was spent checking mileages on every available map. By morning I was convinced that the distances and directions of travel cited in the diaries indicated that Frémont had not been on the Rio Grande above Monte Vista, Colorado. Handing my completed, but inaccurate, paper to the professor, I explained my newly formed hypothesis. He looked at me and said, "That's what I've always thought. Now, prove it!" Had I realized that December day in 1968 that "proving it" would take twenty years, I might have reconsidered.

Successfully retracing Frémont's route into the San Juan Mountains required both academic research and extensive field work. Acquiring access to documents and the cooperation of agencies and individuals was an easy task. Following mountain trails and checking timberline for campsites proved a tougher assignment.

The San Luis Valley, which was the scene of disaster for Frémont's fourth expedition into the uncharted West, is the largest of Colorado's four intermountain basins or "parks." The virtually treeless plain is surrounded by mountains: the volcanic San Juan Range lies to the west; the spectacular Sangre de Cristo Mountains, with peaks over 14,000 feet, form the eastern boundary. Although the San Luis Valley lies along the same lines of latitude as states with moderate climates, the bowl shape entraps cold air and creates a deep-freeze effect with severe winter temperatures. This environment can be as formidable today as it was in 1848-49.

Responsibility for the failure of the fourth expedition has been a favorite topic of writers ever since Frémont continued to California with sixteen survivors, leaving a half dozen men, including his guide Bill Williams, in Taos, New Mexico. Generally aware of the area in which the expedition faced disaster, biographers and historians made little effort to identify the exact route Frémont and his men followed until Mr. and Mrs. Albert Pfeiffer, Jr., of Monte Vista, Colorado, discovered tall stumps and two abandoned sledges on the slopes of Mesa Mountain. With renewed interest, historians and popular writers began proposing possible routes to the Rincon Creek camp.

Few historians writing about the fourth expedition have been to the sites identified by the Pfeiffers. Frank Spencer, professor of history at the newly established Adams State Normal School in Alamosa, Colorado, was the first historian to visit the area. Pfeiffer took Spencer and forest ranger E. S. Ericson to the camps in 1928. Spencer later shared information with historian Raymond Settle, who packed into the area in 1939. William Brandon also visited the camp identified as the Christmas Camp by the U.S. Forest Service. Most historians have relied upon the work of other writers when describing the route; therefore, a misinterpretation by one sometimes has become accepted as fact by several.

While camped at Big Timbers in eastern Colorado, Frémont wrote to his father-in-law, Missouri's Senator Thomas Hart Benton, that he intended to "ascend the Del Norte to its head, descend on to the Colorado, and so across the Wahsatch mountains and the basin country somewhere near the 37th parallel" (Hafen and Hafen, *Frémont's Fourth Expedition*, 76-77). Analysis of the fourth expedition's route into the La Garita Mountains depends upon the interpretation of "ascend the Del Norte to its head." Two factors are important in determining the meaning of this phrase: What information would Frémont have known about the San Luis Valley and what can the writings of other explorers and early settlers reveal about "the valley of the Rio del Norte"?

Few explorers had preceded Frémont into the San Luis Valley. Only one, New Mexico's Governor Juan Bautista de Anza, had acquired much cartographical information. Determined to stop constant raiding by the Comanches, Anza led an expedition of settlers and Indian allies northward through the San Luis Valley to Poncha Pass and then followed the drainages of the Arkansas River. After intercepting and defeating Cuerno Verde and his marauding band near present Rye, Colorado, the expedition reentered the San Luis Valley over Sangre de Cristo Pass and returned to Taos and Santa Fe.

The only American explorer entering the San Luis Valley before Frémont was Lieutenant Zebulon Montgomery Pike in January 1807. Pike was exploring the southwestern boundaries of the Louisiana Purchase when he trespassed onto the frontier of New Spain while seeking relief for his men. The only map of the San Luis Valley available to Pike was the Miera y Pacheco map of 1779, which drew upon information provided by the Anza expedition. In the Miera y Pacheco map the Rio Grande del Norte flows from the north, as would befit its name, along a course resembling today's San Luis-Saguache drainages. The river appears elongated so as to give Spain claim to greater expanses of territory in the courts of Europe, but the relationships of the San Luis Valley to the upper Arkansas valley and of the Rio Grande and its tributaries are accurate.

Although official exploration of the area surrounding the headwaters of the Rio Grande del Norte was limited, mountain men, trappers, and prospectors had traversed the San Luis Valley and surrounding mountains for decades. Three such men, known by Frémont, resided in Taos. Antoine Robidoux had taken wagons across a pass at the south end of the sand hills since the 1820s. The route bore his name--Robidoux's Road. Antoine Leroux had hauled supplies by wagon through the Cochetopa country to a trading fort on the Uncompahgre River. Kit Carson, Frémont's close friend and guide during his first three expeditions, had trapped extensively in the mountains surrounding the San Luis Valley. The Taos or Trappers' Trail, connecting the plains of Colorado with the northern New Mexican settlements, also was known as Kit Carson's Trail.

During Frémont's third expedition a small party led by Carson had examined Poncha Pass and the complex of passes known as the Cochetopa while Frémont and the rest of the expedition explored the upper Arkansas valley. Carson's reconnaissance of the northern mountains of the San Luis Valley provided information for Frémont's cartographer, Charles Preuss, in preparing his 1848 *Map of Oregon and Upper California*, which included the Cochetopa region.

In 1814 explorer William Clark combined information gathered during the explorations of the Louisiana Territory with the Miera y Pacheco map to create a strange distortion of the West that omitted all of Wyoming and Colorado north of the Platte River. On this map Colter's River in the Yellowstone country is shown as a tributary of the Rio Grande. Even so, Clark's map represented the most up-to-date and detailed portrait of southern Colorado and northern New Mexico.

There can be little doubt that Frémont knew the characteristics of the passes through the mountains surrounding the San Luis Valley or that he intended to use the most open and easily accessible, the Cochetopa, to reach the tributaries of the Colorado River. The location of the complex near the 38th parallel made it ideal for a central route to California. Frémont declared, ''Our examinations around the southern headwaters of the Arkansas, have made us acquainted with many

passes, grouped together in a small space of country, con-
ducting by short and practicable valleys from the waters of
the Arkansas just described, to the valleys of the *Del Norte*
and East Colorado" (Spence, *The Expeditions of John Charles
Frémont*, 482).

Having considered the extent of Frémont's knowledge of
the San Luis Valley prior to the fourth expedition, we must
ask the next question: What did Frémont mean by "ascend
the Del Norte to its head"? He had no records or maps that
would have allowed the kind of intimate knowledge available today; however, if we examine the course of the Rio
Grande from the San Juan Mountains of Colorado to the Gulf
of Mexico, it becomes obvious that the entire San Luis Valley
with all its streams forms the headwaters of this great river.

In 1853 both Captain John W. Gunnison, leader of the
official expedition surveying a possible railroad route through
the San Luis Valley, and Solomon Carvalho, who was a member
of Frémont's fifth expedition, described the San Luis Valley
as the headwaters of the Rio Grande. After participating in
a bear hunt on Mosca Pass, Carvalho wrote, "I had the first
view into the San Louis [*sic*] Valley, the head waters of the
'Rio Grande del Norte'" (*Incidents of Travel and Adventure in
the Far West*, 139).

Considering all of the San Luis Valley as the headwaters
of the Rio Grande and the Cochetopa complex as Frémont's
objective, what river did he and his men encounter? The
"del Norte," as identified by Frémont, Gunnison, and Carvalho, was the Saguache River, a major tributary of the Rio
Grande. During the 1800s, before drought and irrigation
changed the landscape, the waters of the Saguache and the
San Luis rivers were significant. As late as 1870, George
Gwyther, surgeon at Fort Garland, noted that settlers of the
San Luis Valley considered the Saguache River to be the
headwater of the Rio Grande.

Determining the meaning of "ascend the Del Norte" has
contributed greatly to retracing the fourth expedition's route
into the La Garita Mountains by allowing a more accurate

interpretation of the mileages, geographic features, and events presented in the diaries, letters, and reminiscences of the members of the ill-fated expedition.

In the years of America's "Manifest Destiny," any man who could write kept a daily record as though that made him part of the nation's course toward greatness. Several members of the fourth expedition followed this custom. Best known are the diaries of Richard and Benjamin Kern. Micajah McGehee's journal, which lay on a shelf for years, is another major source of information about the expedition. Charles Preuss's diary, which surfaced in Germany, has answered many questions about the events of those winter months of 1848-49.

Apparently some diaries have been lost. Richard Kern wrote to Andrew Cathcart and asked for his journal, but there is no indication it was received. Oddly, Edward Kern's diary ends in October 1848, before the expedition entered the mountains. J. H. Simpson, a West Point graduate and contemporary of Frémont, asked Edward for his diary. Simpson, who denounced the idea of a transcontinental railroad, first claiming one could never be built and later stating it would never be practicable to carry passengers, tried repeatedly to discredit Frémont as an explorer. Edward Kern may have sent part of his diary to Simpson, or he may have destroyed those pages that caused him the greatest distress. Other members who reportedly had journals were Henry King, Charles Taplin, and Bill Williams.

Most certainly Frémont would have kept a daily journal. His wife Jessie may have helped write the reports that led to Frémont's popularity, but the descriptive narratives that made easterners yearn to see the West came from careful notations made during each journey. Frémont's diary has disappeared, but historian Frank Spencer claimed he saw and read it while visiting in Washington, D.C. Frémont's firsthand account surely would clarify many controversial aspects of the fourth expedition.

In 1853 Frémont returned to the San Luis Valley. Following the expeditions of John W. Gunnison and E. F. Beale, Frémont's fifth expedition found little snow on Cochetopa Pass. A short time later this party, stranded by a blizzard, was forced to butcher its horses. One man died, apparently of pneumonia. Eventually the expedition reached the Mormon settlements and continued to California. Notes, letters, and reports to Congress concerning the fifth expedition shed light on the route Frémont intended to follow in 1848-49.

Alexis Godey, whom Frémont described as a young Kit Carson, left no journal; but in a letter written to vindicate Frémont of charges leveled during the 1856 presidential campaign, Godey provided the key to identifying the route of the fourth expedition by referring repeatedly to the "Carnero." The issue in 1856 was not where the expedition met with disaster, but who was responsible, Frémont or Williams, and whether Frémont had abandoned some of his men in New Mexico. Godey was not without prejudice. He had served with Frémont on several expeditions and had become a close friend of the Pathmarker; but if any man knew the trail of the expedition, it was Godey. He had piloted the expedition across the sand hills, led King's party to the Rio Grande, accompanied Frémont to the New Mexican settlements, and returned with relief for the survivors.

Confirmation of the Carnero route began as early as 1859, when Domicio Espinosa, Susano Trujillo, and Cornelio Abeyta began grazing sheep on the slopes of Mesa Mountain. At least one of the herders had been with Godey's relief party and knew the story of the disastrous ascent into the mountains. Finding campsites with tall stumps, charred rock ledges, a rock with writing on it, a military jacket, the skeletons of mules, and other artifacts, these men passed the stories to their descendants. Eventually the locations of the inscribed rock and the camps became part of family folklore as the Rincon Creek stumps and sledges overshadowed the discoveries of the La Garita settlers.

Final evidence for the route of John C. Frémont's fourth expedition came in 1982. While attending a Gran Quivira conference in New Mexico, historian David Weber, who had been commissioned to write a biography of Richard H. Kern, one of the expedition's artists, produced photographs of some of Kern's watercolors of the San Luis Valley. It was an exciting day for me as the watercolors depicted quite accurately scenes that had become familiar throughout the many years I had spent retracing the route.

In 1958 many sketches, watercolors, and manuscripts by the Kern brothers were found in the basement of the Belleview Hotel, Dingman's Ferry, Pennsylvania. Part of the collection appeared in *Life* magazine in 1959. The Amon Carter Museum, Fort Worth, Texas, purchased another twenty-one watercolors and four pencil sketches in 1975. David Weber's *Richard H. Kern: Expeditionary Artist in the Far Southwest, 1848-1853* contains plates of the Amon Carter collection and other Kern works, which were exhibited throughout the western states in 1985.

Many of the problems historians have faced in trying to determine the exact route of the expedition of 1848-49 resulted from a lack of sufficient knowledge of the San Luis Valley. Residency provides an insight that cannot be acquired through reading or short visits. Knowing geographic features, understanding weather patterns, locating reputable people with personal or family histories, and having time and opportunity to check and recheck details are essential for an accurate interpretation of Frémont's route.

Because this retracing of the route of the fourth expedition is not traditional, I covered the entire area more than once in all seasons and all kinds of weather. I traversed mountains, valleys, passes, rivers, and trails by four-wheel-drive vehicle, snowmobile, horseback, snowshoes, and cross-country skis; but most commonly by foot or "shanks' mare" while bearing a pack laden with cameras, lenses, film, books, maps, notepads, and the necessary survival gear. I made many trips to adjoining areas to assure myself that the evidence was not coincidental. The diaries, reminiscences, oral histories, stumps, eroded dates, and mule bones fit together like clues in a Sherlock Holmes mystery. The cement binding all the pieces together was Richard Kern's watercolors.

The purpose of this trail guide is not to provide another biography of John C. Frémont or another history about the fourth expedition and the national events that spurred the transcontinental railroad surveys. Numerous authors, listed in the bibliography, already have dealt with those topics. *Trail to Disaster* is a guide for modern explorers who enjoy a sense of camaraderie with past generations. The pages that follow, detailing specifically the fourth expedition's trail to disaster, are for adventurous disciples of America's history and heritage.

Patricia Joy Richmond

---

THIS TRAIL guide of the route of John C. Frémont's fourth expedition has received support and assistance from many people. First, I wish to remember the late Pauline (Pat) Sharp of Monte Vista, Colorado, who encouraged me constantly. She accompanied me during those first excursions up Cave Creek and allowed me to use information and materials collected by her father, historian Raymond W. Settle.

The late Barbara Colville of Del Norte, Colorado, was my guide and companion on many trips to the Frémont camps. From her I learned how to cross-country ski, climb a mountain, and live in the wilderness.

Historians Mary Lee Spence and David Weber gave me professional guidance and the reassurances I needed when the project, especially the completion of this manuscript, seemed overwhelming. I am most grateful.

Technical assistance came from many sources. Rio Grande National Forest personnel, especially Russ Schwulst and Joe Hartman, helped me with maps and trail identification. Gene Huser of Monte Vista, Colorado, and Marlene Pruitt of Crestone, Colorado, gave the assistance needed to get the manuscript on the computer. Dr. and Mrs. Richard Beidleman of Colorado Springs, Colorado, who have been retracing the route of Captain John W. Gunnison, read the Frémont manuscript and offered sound advice. I am also indebted to Charles Elliott, Carl Keck, the late George Ward, and Frank White for sharing their recollections with me and all those who follow this guide.

Many staff members in the library at Adams State College have assisted me in locating source material over the years of my research. I am also indebted to my editor, David Wetzel, whose skills and concern for accuracy have helped to assure that the quality of this volume justifies the many years spent researching the trail of the fourth expedition.

Of course, family and friends have been faithful in supporting this twenty-year project. Ruth Marie Colville of Del Norte, Colorado, has been my gadfly. Her questionings required careful research and definitive answers. The late Helen G. Blumenschein of Taos, New Mexico, helped by calling attention to passages that would confuse people unfamiliar with the San Luis Valley.

I have shared many hours on horseback with my friend Sondra Schwulst since she first taught me how to ride. The new forest ranger and his staff, who wanted to see the Frémont sites, never knew how frightened I was coming off Mesa Mountain on the back of a beast; but constantly thinking that the next hundred yards were "no farther than Mexican Hill," where Sondra had taught me equestrian skills in four hours, and accepting that her aged mountain horse Marg knew what to do carried me through the ordeal in fine form.

While the length of time spent researching this work has been extensive, a desire to procrastinate--to check one more source, to climb one more hill, to ski up one more valley, to examine one more copse of trees--attests to the pleasure that has come from walking in the footsteps of John C. Frémont and the men of the fourth expedition.

I developed a love of history as a child. No fiction was as fascinating as the true stories shared with me by my parents, John A. (Jack) and Lillian Anderson. Their lives reflected the historic events described in my school texts.

My son Paul has admonished often, "Mom, when are you going to finish Frémont?" I have completed this guide for him. One day I realized that I had worked on this project for two thirds of his life--that I was a young woman when I started tracking Frémont and his men through the San Juan Mountains. Then it occurred to me that following Frémont had kept me young in spirit by giving me knowledge, skills, and adventures I would not have acquired otherwise. May all who follow the trail of the fourth expedition find the experience as rewarding.

*Pike's Peak 1848 ('Mon Songe').* Watercolor by Richard H. Kern. Courtesy Amon Carter Museum, Fort Worth, Texas.

## NOTE

The route of John Charles Frémont's fourth expedition can be followed approximately by vehicle, but an accurate retracing is available only to those who leave the highways and roads and follow the trails used for centuries by animals, nomads, and explorers. To recognize names, dates, and places is to know history; to walk the paths used by our ancestors is to understand heritage.

This trail guide is designed for use with Carson, Rio Grande, and San Isabel national forest maps which are available at area Forest Service headquarters. Standard Colorado and New Mexico road maps will identify national and state highways mentioned in the guide.

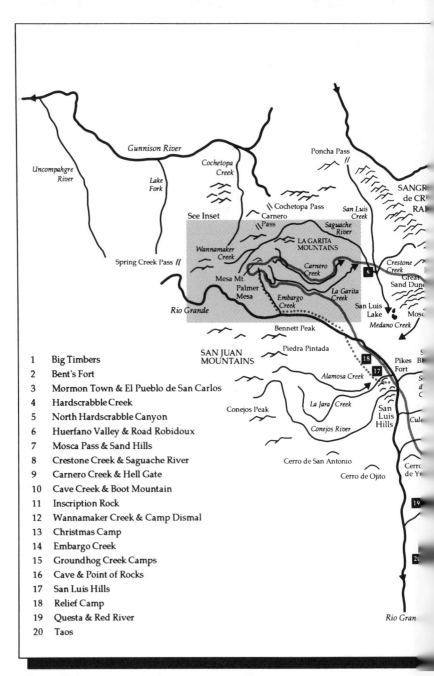

1   Big Timbers
2   Bent's Fort
3   Mormon Town & El Pueblo de San Carlos
4   Hardscrabble Creek
5   North Hardscrabble Canyon
6   Huerfano Valley & Road Robidoux
7   Mosca Pass & Sand Hills
8   Crestone Creek & Saguache River
9   Carnero Creek & Hell Gate
10  Cave Creek & Boot Mountain
11  Inscription Rock
12  Wannamaker Creek & Camp Dismal
13  Christmas Camp
14  Embargo Creek
15  Groundhog Creek Camps
16  Cave & Point of Rocks
17  San Luis Hills
18  Relief Camp
19  Questa & Red River
20  Taos

Route of John C. Frémont's Fourth Expedition, 1848-1849

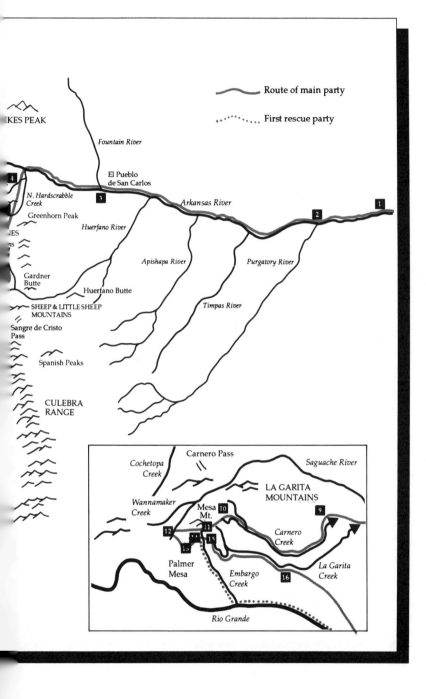

Route of main party

First rescue party

IKES PEAK

Fountain River

El Pueblo
de San Carlos

4

3

N. Hardscrabble
Creek

Arkansas River

2

1

Greenhorn Peak

IES

ns

Huerfano River

Apishapa River

Purgatory River

Gardner
Butte

Huerfano Butte

SHEEP & LITTLE SHEEP
MOUNTAINS

Timpas River

Sangre de Cristo
Pass

Spanish Peaks

CULEBRA
RANGE

Carnero Pass

Cochetopa
Creek

Saguache River

LA GARITA
MOUNTAINS

Wannamaker
Creek

Mesa 10
Mt.

9

12

11

Carnero
Creek

14 15

13

Palmer
Mesa

Embargo
Creek

16

La Garita
Creek

Rio Grande

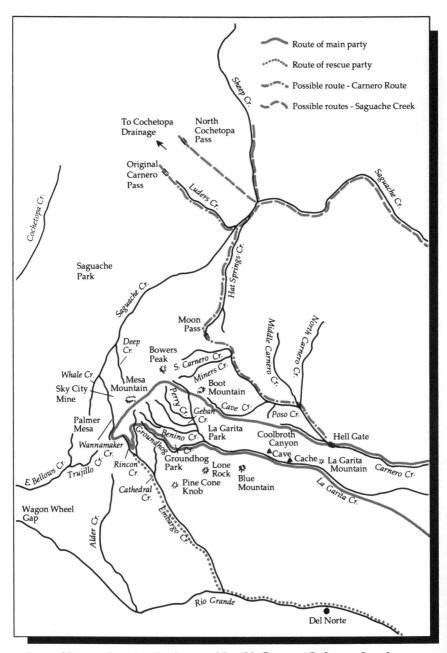

Route of Frémont Party into San Juans and Possible Routes to Cochetopa Complex

*Robidoux' Pass, White Mountains, N.M., 1848* [North Hardscrabble Canyon].
Watercolor by Richard H. Kern. Courtesy Amon Carter Museum, Fort Worth, Texas.

*On Proulx' Creek, Chowatch Mountains., N.M., 1849.* Watercolor by Richard H. Kern. Courtesy Amon Carter Museum, Fort Worth, Texas.

Cave Creek Site, 1985. Courtesy Patricia Joy Richmond.

Engraving for Prospectus for *Memoirs of My Life* [Camp Dismal on Wannamaker Creek with High Peaks of San Juan Mountains in Background] Courtesy Huntington Library

View from Summit of Boot Mountain toward High Peaks of San Juan Mountains. Courtesy Patricia Joy Richmond

*Relief Camp on the Rio Grande del Norte, N.M., Jan. 29, 1848* [1849]. Watercolor by Richard H. Kern. Courtesy Amon Carter Museum, Fort Worth, Texas.

Sierra Blanca from the Rio Grande south of Alamosa near site of Relief Camp, 1985. Courtesy Patricia Joy Richmond.

# Trail to Disaster

O N TUESDAY, October 3, 1848, John C. Frémont and thirty-five men left St. Louis, Missouri, bound for California. Most of the men were veterans of previous expeditions; the rest were seeking adventure in the fabled West.[1] The objective of the expedition was the exploration of a central railroad route to the Pacific. The goal was never achieved. Two months later men and mules struggled to survive in the snow-covered wilderness of the La Garita Mountains in southern Colorado.[2]

Frémont had intended to follow as closely as possible an all-seasons route between the 37th and 38th parallels. He had been advised that good passes through the Rocky Mountains and Sierra Nevada could be found near these latitudes.[3] The route was feasible, the expedition well outfitted, the men eager. No one anticipated the suffering and horror that the men soon would endure. Yet carelessness was not the cause of the miseries that befell Frémont and his men. The ruin of the expedition resulted primarily because unusually severe early winter storms swept across mountains normally snow-free until late December, and an incessant southwest wind sent temperatures plummeting to well below zero.[4]

## BIG TIMBERS

The expedition had crossed Kansas and reached Chouteau's Island on the Arkansas River by November 8, 1848.[5] The only problems encountered en route had been a prairie fire and a blizzard. Proceeding along the Arkansas, the men reached Big Timbers near the present site of Lamar, Colorado. The 600 lodges of Apache, Arapaho, Comanche, and Kiowa, wintering at Big Timbers when Frémont arrived November 12, 1848, attested to the excellent protection provided by this extensive cottonwood grove, which stood one mile wide according to Micajah McGehee. Thomas ("Brokenhand") Fitzpatrick, who had served with Frémont as a guide during the third expedition, was the Indian agent at Big Timbers. McGehee observed that the Indians, camped at the eastern edge of the timber, had many children with them whom they had stolen from the New Mexican settlements to the south.

Frémont and several of the men enjoyed the hospitality extended them, but Edward Kern was disgusted by the "children of Nature." Some of the Indians at Big Timbers advised Frémont of the early, deep snows in the mountains; however, such information was not likely to deter men used to facing hardships, overcoming obstacles, or achieving the impossible. In fact, Ben Kern noted that a little snow was refreshing after the uncomfortably warm winds of the Kansas prairie.

---

McGehee gave the distance from Big Timbers to Bent's Fort as eighty-five miles. Traveling along the south bank of the Arkansas River, the expedition crossed a stream, identified as the Whetstone, fifteen miles below the fort. Five miles farther west was the Purgatoire River. Private property makes it difficult to follow exactly the route taken from Big Timbers to Bent's Fort, but U.S. Highway 50 west, though located on the north side of the river from Lamar to Las Animas, is in proximity.

## BENT'S FORT

Charles and William Bent built their first trading fort at the mouth of the Fountain River. Eventually they abandoned that fort and relocated farther downstream on the north bank of the Arkansas River--still in line with the mountain fur trade but nearer the traffic of the Santa Fe Trail. The second fort, sometimes called Fort William, existed until 1852 when William Bent destroyed it and built a new fort even farther downstream. Charles Bent, appointed governor of New Mexico by General Stephen Watts Kearny, had been murdered during the Taos Rebellion in January 1847.

On November 17 Frémont and his men, in their camp across the river and two miles downstream from Bent's Fort, had an excellent view of Pikes Peak, the drainages of the Huérfano River, including Greenhorn Mountain, and the Spanish Peaks, once used as landmarks to identify Spanish territory. McGehee, seeing light reflecting from the mountains thoroughly covered with snow, referred to them as "a chilling prospect." That night, McGehee observed that the aurora borealis appeared as "spires of blue and scarlet to the very zenith." Since a storm lasting a night and a day had deposited twelve inches of new snow, the men spent their time writing to friends or adding clothing that would help them endure the colder weather.

A reconstruction of Bent's Fort, completed in 1976 by the National Park Service, can be reached by taking Colorado Highway 194 from Las Animas to La Junta. The park is open daily except Thanksgiving and Christmas.

## MORMONTOWN AND
## EL PUEBLO DE SAN CARLOS

In 1846, as the Mormons were migrating through Wyoming, they learned that the United States was at war with Mexico. A party of young men rode south to join General Kearny's New Mexico campaign. When Kearny left Santa Fe for California, the Mormons decided to rejoin their families to the north. George Frederick Ruxton, having left Taos just days before the fatal uprising during which Charles Bent was murdered, followed the Mormons' trail to El Pueblo in January 1847 and described their journey.[6] The passage through the San Luis Valley provided the Mormons with information that encouraged their settlement of that high mountain park in the 1870s.

Being sick but unwelcome at the adobe fortress El Pueblo de San Carlos, located at the mouth of the Fountain or Boiling Springs River (possibly the site of the Bent brothers' first fort), the Mormons spent the winter in crude log houses that they had built on the south side of the Arkansas River. Apparently some mountain men and their families were occupying the cabins abandoned by the Mormons when Frémont arrived at the site on November 22, 1848. Frémont's men established a camp among cottonwoods away from the animal stench emanating from the tiny community.

According to Charles Preuss's diary, Bill Williams, who was staying at the pueblo across the river, came to Frémont's camp and offered to serve as a guide. Williams claimed to know the mountains to the west better than any man, as he had traversed them for over thirty years. It seems strange that Frémont would hire the old mountaineer considering not only Williams's reputation as a scoundrel but his role as one of several mountaineers who had left Frémont's third expedition near the Great Salt Lake.

Frémont probably would have preferred his guide of previous expeditions, Kit Carson. Carson had just returned to New Mexico from Washington, D.C., in October 1848. Frémont may have learned at Bent's Fort that Carson, Lucien Maxwell, and Robert Fisher had been sent with trade goods to reopen Bent's Fort Apache on the Canadian River. After returning from this unsuccessful attempt to reestablish trade with the Comanches, Carson accompanied Major Benjamin L. Beall on two expeditions in pursuit of hostile Apaches under Chico Velasquez. Carson had been busy throughout the months during which Frémont's expedition attempted to cross the mountains but was at home in Taos when Frémont arrived in late January 1849. Comments attributed to Carson by Jessie Frémont might indicate that he encouraged Frémont in believing that the problems encountered by the fourth expedition were the responsibility of the guide Williams.

A replica of El Pueblo de San Carlos, described by McGehee as a group of adobe houses surrounding a dilapidated fort about seventy miles west of Bent's Fort, has been constructed at El Pueblo Museum in Pueblo, Colorado. U.S. Highway 50 to Pueblo follows the south bank of the Arkansas and crosses the Timpas, Apishapa, Huérfano, and St. Charles rivers, as did Frémont and his men.

## HARDSCRABBLE

The Hardscrabble settlement was founded in 1844 at the confluence of Newlin, Adobe, and Hardscrabble creeks. Approximately twenty-five mountain men with their Indian wives and families lived there when Frémont visited the settlement in 1845.[7] By November 23, 1848, the community had dwindled to twelve houses. McGehee noted that "no one was here" because the residents had moved to the settlements at the confluence of the Fountain and Arkansas rivers after an Indian attack.

At Hardscrabble, Frémont, unconvinced by Williams's statement that the expedition would encounter no snow if they crossed the mountains before Christmas, purchased corn described by McGehee as being the previous year's harvest and of good quality. The mountain men who had accompanied the expedition from El Pueblo and Frémont's men shelled corn day and night until they had sacked 130 bushels--enough to carry the 120 animals through the San Juan Mountains in an emergency. While it has been assumed that Frémont had only mules with him by this time, Ben Kern's diary refers to getting corn for the horses, some of which had been acquired at El Pueblo.

During their brief stay in this frontier community, Frémont and his men enjoyed the homey comforts of table and stools while supping on chicken and pumpkin. Within a few weeks this simplicity would be remembered as a luxury. Frémont did not tarry long in this primitive haven but at midday on November 25 departed on foot, the animals laden with sacks of corn. That day one disgruntled member, Longe, predicted evil to those who continued and left the expedition.

Frémont's route from El Pueblo to Hardscrabble crossed the Arkansas River several times as the men followed what the Kerns described as a "rough route" over hills of yellow sandstone with clay bluffs. The camp west of El Pueblo was along the river's bottom on the north bank. Next morning the expedition left the Arkansas and passed the red hills near present Florence, Colorado. Both Richard and Ben Kern noted that though a cold wind blew from the gap of the Arkansas, the weather was as warm and damp as in April.

Either Colorado Highway 96 or U.S. Highway 50 with Colorado Highway 120 leads from Pueblo to Colorado Highway 67 and the location of Hardscrabble. There is no trace of this "summer resort of hunters," as Richard Kern described it, among the juniper, pine, and oak trees that cover the hills between Florence and Wetmore.

## HARDSCRABBLE CANYON

Another name for Hardscrabble Creek was White Oak Creek in reference to the dense growth of scrub oak along the stream. On the first day after leaving the Hardscrabble settlement, the expedition traveled a short distance, three to four miles, before camping near the present site of Wetmore, Colorado. The next day the men moved eight miles farther past parallel rock walls. As they entered the Rocky Mountains, George Hubbard remarked, "Friends, I don't want my bones to bleach upon those mountains this winter amidst that snow." That evening several men climbed a ridge near camp and from its height saw a lake, possibly Lake San Isabel, reflecting the lights of the night sky. On November 27 Ben Kern made a sketch of Hardscrabble Canyon. Later Richard Kern may have used that sketch to complete the watercolor mislabeled *Robidoux' Pass*, now in the Amon Carter collection.

Williams led the expedition past cliffs, over hills, and through valleys. Camps were made in deep snow. There was no water, a situation that would debilitate the mules faster than the lack of food. The corn, intended for hard times in the San Juans, was fed to the weakening animals as the expedition moved through the Wet Mountains.

Both North and South Hardscrabble creeks offer access into the Wet Mountains and both have impressive canyons. However, the recorded distances and descriptions of multicolored monoliths jutting above the canyon walls, as well as the ascents and descents through snow-filled valleys and the view of the White Mountains (Sierra de Nieve), another name for the northern Sangre de Cristo Range, more aptly identify a route following North Hardscrabble Creek. Turning south, Frémont's trail would have moved between Arkansas Mountain and Rudolph Mountain toward Gobbler's Knob and the headwaters of South Hardscrabble Creek and its tributary, Ophir Creek. Crossing Promontory Divide, the expedition passed onto the headwaters of Williams Creek, a tributary of the Huérfano River. A reference in Ben Kern's diary to aspen trees indicates that the expedition was following a trail reaching elevations near 10,000 feet as it crossed a "bleak, bald ridge."

Colorado Highways 96 and 165, four-wheel-drive (4x4) roads 310 and 401, and the Gardner Road 400 are in proximity to this route, part of which can be traced on foot although there are no official trails through this segment of the San Isabel National Forest. A stage line connecting the mining camps of Silver Park and Keating once followed part of this trail in the early 1860s.

## THE HUERFANO VALLEY
## AND ROAD ROBIDOUX

On November 29, with the Wet Mountains to the north of them, Frémont and his men, exhausted by the up-and-down march through snow, approached the valley of the Huérfano River.[8] Richard Kern noted as they descended toward this east-flowing tributary of the Arkansas that Gardner Butte looked like a fortress or "bastion" at the edge of the Huérfano's wide, meadowed bottom. The "little Spanish Peaks," Sheep Mountain and Little Sheep Mountain, resembling their famous neighbors, the Spanish Peaks, dominated the view to the south.[9] As the expedition rested about ten miles from the gap of the Huérfano, the men replaced their deteriorating boots with moccasins, a step which would help prevent the severe frost-bite suffered by many of Zebulon Pike's men in 1807.

Following Antoine Robidoux's wagon road along the north side of the river, the expedition moved west and camped at the gap of the Huérfano near the present settlement of Red Wing. Here a gigantic twist in the great wall through which the river has cut its channel demonstrates the tremendous forces that once played within these mountains.

The next day the men continued through the canyon of the Huérfano for two and a half miles and then followed the road as it wound over immense piñon-covered hills that hid the 14,000-foot snow-clad peaks of the Sangre de Cristo Mountains. Finding little snow to hinder their ascent, though winds made them uncomfortable, Frémont and his men reached the 9,175-foot summit of Robidoux or Mosca Pass at noon on December 3 and gazed into the "valley of the Rio del Norte"--

the San Luis Valley.[10]  McGehee wrote, "One broad, white, dreary-looking plain lay before us bounded by white mountains."  At the base of the pass were the sand hills, looking exactly as described by Zebulon Pike in 1807.[11]

Colorado Highway 69 from Gardner to Sharpsdale and 4x4 Road 407 follow a route similar to Road Robidoux to the summit of Mosca Pass.  Wagon ruts, initiated by Robidoux and deepened by homesteaders and miners using the toll road to cross the pass in the late 1800s, still are visible at the summit.

## MOSCA PASS
## AND THE SAND HILLS

The Mosca Creek trail into the San Luis Valley passed huge blocks of "naked rock" as it cut through a narrow, steep canyon choked with fallen timber.  In spite of the four and a half feet of snow on the road and eight feet in the gullies, the men reported a warm, easy day.  Camp was made among junipers by a small stream, Médano Creek, south of the sand hills near the modern Pinyon Flats campground of the Great Sand Dunes National Monument. With night came winds, snow, and bitter cold reported by McGehee to be seventeen degrees below zero.  Some of the men pitched tents for protection.

The next day, December 5, the expedition tried to move between the sand hills and the mountains, but the extremely cold temperature, deep snow, and wind impeded any progress.  Meanwhile Frémont, Creutzfeldt, King, Preuss, and Williams examined the gap of Médano Pass.  Preuss wondered about the long, difficult, provision-exhausting detour and considered it odd that Williams had avoided using this "real pass," sometimes identified by the old mountaineer's name. Had the expedition followed North Hardscrabble Creek to its source and then crossed into the Wet Mountain Valley, the men would have reached Médano Pass approximately two days after leaving Hardscrabble.  The route over Mosca Pass had taken over a week, had depleted the supplies, and had seriously taxed the energies of men and animals.[12]

The third day after entering the San Luis Valley, with a noon temperature still below zero, Alexis Godey finally led the expedition directly over the crest of the sand hills, which were covered with up to six feet of snow. Historians, ignoring the significance of the repeated attempts to pass to the north end of the dunes, have assumed that Frémont moved directly from the sand hills to the Rio Grande. Had Frémont wanted to follow the main branch of the Rio Grande into the San Juan Mountains, he could have reached that river easily from his camp at the south end of the dunes as Zebulon Pike had done in 1807. The time and effort spent surmounting this granular obstacle indicate that Frémont's goal was the valley of the Saguache River and its access to the Cochetopa complex.

The trail from the summit of Mosca Pass across the Great Sand Dunes is inaccessible to vehicles. Problems associated with pursuing the route through this area should be discussed with national monument personnel. A lithograph of the sand hills, reproduced in Robert Hines's *Edward Kern and American Expansion* (recently reprinted as *In the Shadow of Frémont*), has been attributed to the 1848 expedition; however, the lack of snow and the summer-apparent landscape suggest that the sketch was made by Richard Kern when the Gunnison expedition camped near the dunes in August 1853.

## CRESTONE CREEK AND THE SAGUACHE RIVER

With frosted toes and inch-long icicles hanging from their beards and hair, the men of the fourth expedition reached the sheltering timbers of a small creek north of the sand dunes. The fallen, dry leaves of the numerous cottonwood trees made fine bedding and helped to protect the men from the night's six-below-zero temperature. Several streams that are tributary to San Luis Creek head among the 14,000-foot peaks once known as *les trois Tétons*.[13] In December 1853, after crossing Médano Pass and the sand hills, according to Frémont, the fifth expedition connected "the line of the present expedition with one explored in 1848-49" and camped on Crestone Creek in what was described by Solomon Carvalho as "an immense natural deer-park." The Crestone Creek area is still a haven for deer, antelope, and mountain sheep.

On the morning of December 7, with six inches of snow on the ground, the 1848 expedition proceeded west-north-west toward the "Rio Grande" and the San Juan Mountains thirty-five miles away. After traveling twenty-two miles, the men camped on the sagebrush-covered plain known today as the Alamosa Basin. Five years later, according to Solomon Carvalho, the fifth expedition also "travelled up the San Louis [sic] Valley, crossing the Rio Grande del Norte, and entered the Sarawatch [sic] Valley." Obviously the river being described by these early explorers as the Rio Grande is the Saguache tributary.[14]

In 1853 Captain John W. Gunnison's party camped south of Crestone Creek among the sparse cottonwoods and willows of Chatillon (Cottonwood) Creek, named for a Taos trapper. Lieutenant Beckwith, who filed the official report of the expedition after Gunnison was massacred, recorded in his journal that the "prairie-grass fields" of the Rivière des Trois Tétons (Crestone Creek) led directly toward "the course to the Coochatope [sic] Pass." The Gunnison expedition, having been warned of marshes, moved farther north to Leroux Creek (Rito Alto), named for their guide, the mountain man Antoine Leroux. Beckwith's description of lower Crestone Creek's extensive marshlands clarifies Ben Kern's statement that Frémont's 1848 expedition passed through a "low place of long grass weeds & cattails."

The six to eight inches of moisture received annually on the 8,000-foot-high floor of the San Luis Valley would be too scant to produce the wetlands encountered by Frémont and his men. Mountain waters, draining into subterranean aquifers within the basin, percolate upward through alluvium to produce numerous artesian springs, shallow lakes, and marshes. High humidity resulting from trans-evaporation of these surface waters, combined with extremely cold night temperatures, often twenty to thirty degrees below zero, creates a morning phenomenon witnessed by the men of the fourth expedition--clouds of ice particles settle into low areas and river bottoms, and long fingers of frost cling to trees, grasses, and brush, enveloping the world in a crystalline shroud. Three days of this pristine whiteness caused Ben Kern to describe the fantastic scene as "dismal."[15]

As the air cleared on the second day into the plain, the men saw trees seven miles to the south. Frémont wanted to continue toward the Saguache Valley, but Williams insisted they would regain lost time by using the Carnero Creek access to the Cochetopa country. Williams's assertion of a shorter route would be correct if a traveler came from the New Mexican settlements. Following the Indian trail along the western edge of the San Luis Valley, wagons had to proceed to the Saguache Valley to cross into Cochetopa Park; however, a person traveling by foot or horse could save at least two days by turning up Carnero Creek. This shortcut ascended the south fork of Carnero Creek to Moon Pass, then descended onto the headwaters of the Saguache. The trail then entered Luders Canyon about one mile upstream from the gateway to Cochetopa Pass, crossed Carnero Pass, and continued along the south side of Cochetopa Dome before connecting with the Cochetopa Pass road to the Lake Fork and Uncompahgre River.

By the 1870s, as wagon travel increased, settlers approached both Carnero and Cochetopa passes from the Saguache Valley. The Carnero Creek access was lost to memory. Carnero Pass became known as Lawrence's Road. The route over Cochetopa Pass was called Mears's Road. Eventually the southern pass of the Cochetopa complex, the old Carnero Pass, was renamed Cochetopa Pass by Forest Service engineers. Cochetopa or Buffalo Pass became North Pass until local protests caused the name to be changed again to North Cochetopa.[16]

Had Frémont followed either the Carnero or the Saguache route, the expedition would have been in Cochetopa Park and on its way to California as Williams had promised. Instead, the men found themselves on the ridges of Mesa Mountain hundreds of feet above their destination. The Cochetopa was so near, yet so inaccessible. While all the trails chosen by Williams did lead to the regions Frémont wanted to cross, it appears now that the old guide selected the worst possible routes to reach the fourth expedition's objectives. Whether the ensuing delays and difficulties were intentional may never be known. One point is obvious--the mules, receiving only a pint of corn twice a day, had passed their levels of endurance before the expedition entered the San Juans. Success had disappeared with each bushel of corn consumed in the Sangre de Cristo Mountains. (See map, p. xxviii.)

Saguache County Road T crosses the floor of the San Luis Valley to the west-northwest of Crestone Creek. The Saguache River, which Gunnison described as being eighteen feet wide in 1853, today disappears into the light, dusty silts surrounding Moffat, Colorado, as the extent of the river's flow has been reduced by modern irrigating techniques.[17] Scant remnants of timber remain to mark the course of the river as the once-forested stream, flowing across an otherwise treeless plain, was denuded by travelers, miners, and homesteaders seeking wood for campfires, cabins, and fences. Road T intersects with U.S. Highway 285, which leads south to the former drainage of Carnero Creek, its trees cleared and its waters now captured by the Rio Grande Canal.[18]

## CARNERO CREEK AND HELL GATE

While modern usage of *carnero* translates as *sheep*, an archaic meaning of this Spanish word was *burial place*. The name *Rio de Carnero,* used officially in 1779 by Juan Bautista de Anza, may have applied to the Indian burial ground at the mouth of Carnero Canyon. In 1855, during the Fort Massachusetts campaign against the Ute Indians, Colonel Thomas Fauntleroy described the site as being littered with skeletal remains. Pictographs, located on rock walls above the burial ground, mark the ancient Indian trail, and a series of gaps cut through various volcanic materials at the entrance of Carnero Canyon.[19]

After a discussion on the plain, Godey and Preuss recommended that Frémont take Williams's advice. Finding two and a half feet of snow in the willows and cottonwoods that once lined the banks of Carnero Creek, Frémont's expedition, moving southwest, walked on the frozen river. Carnero Creek, like its parallel neighbor, La Garita Creek, flows to the northeast after reaching the seemingly level floor of the San Luis Valley. The Saguache and the Rio Grande enigmatically flow southeast across the same plain and then cut south at their oxbows. The extensive timber along La Garita and Carnero creeks caused settlers in the 1860s and 1870s to refer to this area as "the bottoms."

Micajah McGehee noted that "rapid, rough-bottomed, but boggy streams" hampered their progress. Entering the "series of Canons" that mark Carnero Creek's exit from the mountains, the men soon were repulsed at the narrow channel formed by the formidable cliffs of Hell Gate.[20] After Godey and five other hunters secured two elk, one of which was left behind, the expedition crossed to the south bank of the creek and followed a trail over hills sparsely timbered with small piñon trees. Friable "clay" formations containing large boulders, as described by Richard Kern, would refer to the geologic Conejos mudflows prevalent along Carnero Creek and its tributaries.

---

Saguache County Road G west of U.S. Highway 285 leads to the Carnero Creek route. Passing over hills to the south of the stream's first gap, Forest Service (FS) Road 690 leads westward from the community of La Garita, originally named Carnero, through Hell Gate to the confluence of the south fork of the Carnero and its tributary, Cave Creek.

Coolbroth Canyon, which joins the Carnero just west of Hell Gate, appears very similar to Carnero Canyon in its orientation and geologic formations; however, the mouth of Coolbroth Canyon is marked by unusual obelisks composed of highly friable volcanic material, as mentioned in Ben Kern's diary. These oddly shaped formations, resembling dwarfs with hats, are not common to other canyons in the area. Fitting Richard Kern's description, the canyon becomes narrow and steep-sided toward its head. A small park, which feeds Poso Creek, lies between Coolbroth Canyon and the upper valley of Cave Creek.

FS Road 671, a 4x4 road, ascends Coolbroth Canyon from its junction with Carnero Creek west of Hell Gate. The official road continues north along Poso Creek and connects with FS Road 675 at the Poso campground. In Section 8, Township 42 North, Range 4 East (T42N, R4E), a makeshift trail descends from the park at the head of Poso Creek by following the drainage of a small, unnamed west-flowing tributary of Cave Creek. Frémont's men would have moved onto Cave Creek by following the natural contours, just as modern hunters and woodgatherers have done to create this primitive road.

## CAVE CREEK AND BOOT MOUNTAIN

On December 12 the expedition "took up the Wahsatch"--a misinterpretation of Sawatch, the Anglicized spelling of the Ute Indian word *saguache*--and followed the rock-walled, steep-sided valley of Cave Creek (Rio de las Cuevas) into the La Garita Mountains. A sketch of a monolith in Richard Kern's diary and one of his watercolors in the Amon Carter collection accurately depict the physical features of Cave Creek.

The balking mules, stumbling over rocks and burnt timber and floundering in snow fifteen feet deep, were pulled up the mountainside by "riatas" tied to their noses. Gaining 2,000 feet in elevation, the expedition climbed through ponderosa forests toward the headwaters of Cave Creek and the twin-peaked summit assumed to be the dividing ridge; however, the distance traveled each day diminished. Only 300 yards were passed December 13, after an hour and a half of toiling and tugging--a hard day for men and mules.[21] The clear, cold weather and tremendous height of the trail provided the men with a panoramic view of the San Luis Valley, the snowcapped, spectacular Sangre de Cristo Mountains marking the eastern boundary of this great intermountain basin.

After some of the men persistently broke trail for the pack animals through snow described by Ben Kern as being elbow deep while on mule back, the expedition finally reached the rocky, treeless apex of Boot Mountain (which Frank White calls El Bole de las Cuevas); but hopes faded quickly and disappointment mounted as the men, gazing to the west from this "immense bald hill supposed to be the dividing ridge," saw a higher elevation--Mesa Mountain, which they again mistakenly assumed would be the great Continental Divide.

The descent into the valley, which is the headwaters of La Garita Creek on the west side of Boot Mountain, though "rapid and slippery," was easier than the ascent. By sunset all but six of the men and eight mules were in a new camp within the protection of the pines. The mules had little access to food as the snow was four to five feet deep. Ben Kern reported that the weather had been moderate except at the summit of the mountain, but cirrus clouds forecast an approaching storm. By 9:00 P.M. it was snowing.

FS Road 673 follows Cave Creek from its confluence with the south fork of the Carnero to its source high on the east face of Boot Mountain. The upper sections of this road, which can be very muddy, should be attempted only with a 4x4 vehicle. A north fork of Road 673 makes a circle trip to the south fork of the Carnero by way of Miners Creek, while a south road passes beneath Boot Mountain's southern peak into the valley that is the headwaters of La Garita Creek. The middle fork of Road 673, which is the end of vehicular travel on Frémont's route, climbs the mountain, as did the men of the fourth expedition. Leaving this FS road in Section 4, T42N, R4E, Frémont's trail continues toward the treeless saddle between Boot Mountain's twin peaks. From this point can be seen not only the massive summit of Mesa Mountain, the dominant peak in the La Garita range, with the rocky ridge that connects it to the high tableland feeding so many tributaries of the Rio Grande, but also the grandeur of the entire San Luis Basin with its encompassing mountain ranges--the Sawatch, the Sangre de Cristo, the Culebra, the Conejos-- and the bubble volcanoes of the Taos Plateau.

While there are some stumps among the scrag of trees at timberline on the east face of Boot Mountain, they have not been identified as a Frémont camp. The camp at the very head of La Garita Creek in the northwest corner of Section 31, T43N, R4E, however, clearly fits the description in Ben Kern's diary and follows the pattern common to all identified Frémont camps--timberline, a copse of trees detached from the main forest, the west bank of a stream, assuring first light, and tall stumps either hacked or chopped with an upward swing. In 1973 nine stumps, measuring four to eight feet high, were standing in this camp. The cold, dry air at timberline had preserved them for 125 years.

## "INSCRIPTION ROCK" AND MESA MOUNTAIN

On Friday, December 15, the men of the fourth expedition drove their mules up the steep slope that leads from the head of La Garita Creek to the tableland at the head of Perry Creek.[22] From this elevated, open expanse the expedition could have descended onto the headwaters of South Carnero Creek or onto Johns Creek and worked its way back toward routes leading to Carnero or Cochetopa passes; however, Frémont and his men continued to drive their baggage-laden mules three and a half miles toward the snowy summit believed to divide the nation's east- and west-flowing waters. According to Charles Preuss, the men had been convinced by Bill Williams that they had only to cross this mountain to find "a snow-free tableland" which would lead them to the Great Basin and the road to California.

Richard Kern noted that their route across the chain of domes and cirques that marks the beginnings of the tributaries of the Saguache River and the Rio Grande--Deep, Bear, Johns, Perry, Geban, and Benino creeks--would have been beautiful had the weather been clear. Travel was easier because winds keep the high parks and surrounding ridges snow-free. Below, to the north, was the expansive Saguache Park through which the expedition would have passed had Frémont followed the Saguache River to the Cochetopa complex as he had intended. Directly south of the ridge lay La Garita and Groundhog creeks gently coursing through their broad parks toward the San Luis Valley.[23]

One half hour before sunset, the expedition established its new camp a quarter of a mile below the 12,944-foot summit of Mesa Mountain. That evening Ben Kern wrote in his diary that the ordeals of the past two days had devastated the animals. Eight had been lost in the struggle to cross Boot Mountain; seven more, including Godey's mule Dick, had succumbed along the torturous trail to this bleak camp. Ben revealed the presence of the elements that would become the killers of men as well as of mules--cold and wind. The persistent southwest winds of the San Luis Valley can take the chill factor to seventy-five degrees below zero when they blow across a mantle of ice and snow like that encountered by Frémont and his men in the winter of 1848. As Ben Kern stated, prospects for success were "gloomy."

---

The trail from the La Garita camp to the camp at the head of West Benino Creek follows FS Trail 796 to the north through Section 36, T43N, R3E, and continues to the southwest along the La Garita Stock Driveway (FS Trail 787), passing the headwaters of Geban and East Benino creeks. Geban Creek was named by the early La Garita sheepherders for a military-style jacket or *gabán* found at its head. McGehee's description of Bill Williams reveals that the old mountaineer wore a French military jacket over his fringed buckskin shirt.[24]

At the head of Benino Creek where the trail makes a definite turn to the south stands a large outcropping of Fish Canyon tuff. In the winter, snowdrifts twelve to fifteen feet deep cover this great rock's southeast face, but the winds keep the trail snow-free as it follows close to the low southwest face of the rock. Against the flat wall of the southwest face of the outcropping, someone laid rocks to construct a D-shaped structure. While lying within this shelter, protected from the howling wind, that vagabond scratched the year of his wanderings--1848--into the rock's volcanic surface. When this inscription was rediscovered in 1975, part of the "one," the first "eight," the "four"--which was clearest of all the numerals--and the final "eight" were still visible. The eight-inch-high numerals are about three inches above the ground--ankle height. Although the shelter with its dated wall lies right next to the trail, hundreds of travelers have passed by without noticing it.

Early herders told their families that Frémont's men had left an inscription on a rock at the head of Benino Creek, but eventually the exact location and the text were lost. As time and wind wore away the grains of volcanic cement, the inscription faded from memory as it faded from view. Today it is visible only when the light and shadow are exactly right. The best month for viewing is September; the best time of day is between 11:00 A.M. and 1:00 P.M. In other months and at other times of the day there is either too much or too little light on the rock's roughened and highly reflective surface.[25.] "Inscription Rock" lies in the southwest corner of Section 2, T42N, R3E, near the line between Sections 2 and 3.

FS Trail 793 leads to the West Benino camp, in Section 10, just below the summit of the mountain. In winter the gnarled, whitened stumps protrude above the snow. Two stumps are encircled by large living trees. This camp is farther from true timberline than other camps and obviously is located in the first shelter the men could find after their long, agonizing day.

Frémont's men never mentioned the danger of avalanches as they trekked across the mountain ridges, but "Inscription Rock" and the trail to the West Benino camp lie below a potential avalanche area. The great crown of snow that builds on Mesa Mountain continues through the summer as a snowbank visible from the floor of the San Luis Valley. Springs and rivulets percolate throughout slopes covered with lush grasses and mountain flowers. Pika, cheeks bulging with gathered seeds and blossoms, scurry from rock to rock as their high-pitched signals resound through the crystal air. Ptarmigan in brown summer plumage stand motionless and wait for danger to pass while overhead great black ravens with spread wings loop-the-loop on the wind's currents. None of these summer wonders of the high country were witnessed by Frémont's men. For them there were only the constants of wind, snow, and cold.

## WANNAMAKER CREEK AND "CAMP DISMAL"

A rosy sky greeted the explorers on the morning of December 16, but within a short time the air was filled with blowing snow. Some men sent ahead to break a trail used huge mauls made from tree trunks to beat a V-shaped channel through the drifting snow, described by Thomas Martin as eighteen to twenty-five feet deep. This was the most difficult day the expedition had faced. The temperature was twenty degrees below zero. The icy blasts froze fingers, feet, ears, and noses. The stupor of hypothermia affected judgments. Charles Preuss related that even the experienced old guide Williams lay down and "wanted to die" at the summit. The view that day truly must have been one of "desolation" as the trail was littered with fallen packs and saddles--the pads as well as blankets, ropes, coats, manes, and tails having been devoured during the night by the starving animals. Dying mules lay gasping where they had collapsed while others, frenzied by stress, exhaustion, and hunger, rushed wildly from the trail and plunged from the ridge into snow-filled depressions, some of which were estimated by McGehee to be one hundred feet deep. The mules' bleached, honeycombed, lichen-covered bones still lie along the terraces at the head of Groundhog Creek and across the ridge that divides Embargo and Rincon creeks from the waters of Wannamaker Creek.[26]

The devastating force of the wind proved too powerful for men and beasts. According to McGehee, the men, admitting defeat after "frequent ineffectual attempts" to pass along the ridge, retreated from this "lofty and dreary solitude" and returned to their previous camp. The Kern brothers huddled within their blanket shelter that night as the "furious" wind and snow continued. Richard Kern stated that a half hour more on the summit of the mountain would have brought about the total destruction of the party, while Ben Kern noted it was a day that "tried the stoutest hearts" and that a few days would bring "deliverance or destruction."

As the day cleared on Sunday, December 17, the men headed directly over the hill instead of trying to follow the southwest ridge of the mountain. The weather was warmer, as the wind had diminished. The first shelter reached was a point of trees just beneath the cornice formed on Bole de Hilda, the dome-shaped summit marking the head of Wannamaker Creek. Some members of the expedition, believing that their efforts finally had brought them to the headwaters of the Colorado River, made their way farther into the trees where a camp was established in four and a half feet of snow. Actually, the expedition had reached one of the headwaters of the Saguache River. This misconception by Frémont and his men exemplifies the truly tragic nature of the expedition--in spite of extensive suffering and losses, they were far from their goal, the

Continental Divide and the western slope of the Rockies.

While most of the men waited in this camp, Charles Preuss and a few others tried to break trail toward a road winding from the west. Although there are no descriptions of camps made by this scouting party as it attempted to cross Palmer Mesa, stumps at the head of Trujillo Creek may be associated with this group, which stopped in a "small fir grove." After days of plodding through snow with "indescribable effort," Preuss wrote that since all "ahead . . . was white, we decided to return." The effect of this action upon the camp is revealed in Ben Kern's diary: "They returned, they returned."

A blizzard buffeted the expedition for several days. Each morning the men used tin plates to scrape six to eight inches of new snow from their beds. The wind, snow, and cold continued. A miserable Ben Kern, eyes blinded by smoke from the campfire, and hair and clothing frozen together by water dripping from a half-erected tent, succumbed to feelings of "horror desolation despair." The impact of his comrades' failure to find a way off the mountain was so great that he made no entries in his diary from December 19 until December 22, when Frémont decided to move the expedition to the south side of the mountain. During this time Richard Kern kept busy by making moccasins while other members of the expedition tried to save the baggage and some of the animals.

The Kerns, Micajah McGehee, Thomas Martin, and Charles Preuss all referred to the plight of the mules, whose plaintive brays echoed across the frozen expanses of the mountain. The surviving animals--fifty-nine were left as of December 20--had been driven to what appeared to be grass protruding through the snow, but the boon was found to be the tips of willows. In this high country the willows, or buckbrush, grow to heights of three to eight feet--an indication that even upon the windblown slopes, which are often snow-free, there was an unusual amount of snow that winter. Without sustenance and exposed to the full fury of the bitter winter winds, most of the mules died upon the ridge above Wannamaker

Creek. (In October 1942 George Ward, a Saguache, Colorado, deputy game warden who was checking hunting licenses, rode from Whale Creek to the head of Wannamaker Creek with his friend Ray Shellabarger. In the stadiumlike cirque below the ridge that feeds the headwaters of Wannamaker Creek, in Section 19, T42N, R3E, they found the snow-white skeletons of Frémont's pack animals. In the meadow at the bottom of the swale, the men built a cairn with the numerous bones and skulls. When Ward returned to the site in June 1943, the bones were gone. During World War II, sugar factories bought prairie-dried bones, which were pulverized and used to bleach sugar. Though Ward's tribute to Frémont and his expedition was dismantled by bonepickers, a large tooth or vertebra occasionally emerges from the grass.)

The rest of the ramada, strung across the mountain, did not die in one night or in one place; thus, their remains are found upon several ridges or in the swales where spring melt, rushing from the great windblown drifts, has carried them bone by bone. While some members of the expedition butchered frozen carcasses for food, others, not wanting to expend the extra effort needed to cut the solidified meat, began slaughtering the debilitated but living animals. Preuss noted that the butchered mules were not thin; therefore, he concluded, they had died from cold and exposure rather than from starvation. According to Ben Kern, one mule named Polly was brought into "Camp Dismal" with hopes of saving her, but Preuss claimed that she, too, was used until her end to drag baggage.

During the 1848 expedition neither Frémont nor his men seemed to realize that conservation of the mules might have meant the difference between the destruction or salvation of the expedition; however, Frémont must have learned something about survival techniques from the ordeals faced by the fourth expedition. When the fifth expedition was trapped by deep snow, Carvalho reported that Frémont allowed only one animal to be slaughtered every six days with each man being allotted a portion of meat to last throughout that period. Many consumed their shares immediately and then hungered for several days, but through careful rationing, Frémont and his Indian guides always had meat. Carvalho also noted that the men of the fifth expedition realized that the animals were their last hope and walked as much as possible.

---

The trail into the Wannamaker camp follows FS Trail 787 from West Benino Creek across the south face of Mesa Mountain and continues toward the southwest to Section 29, T42N, R3E, where it intersects FS Trail 908, which leads directly to the head of Wanna-maker Creek. "Camp Dismal," as Ben Kern called it, is located just below the ridge in the easternmost stand of the three circular groves of trees on the west side of Wannamaker Creek at the intersection of Sections 19, 20, 29, and 30, T42N, R3E. The first stumps were among the highest point of timber just below the summit of Bole de Hilda, where blowing snow would form cornices and deep drifts. In 1928 Charles Elliott visited this site with his grandfather, Albert Pfeiffer, Jr. Elliott, who was twelve years old, could not reach the tops of the tallest stumps while standing on horseback. These stumps, now fallen, measure from sixteen to thirty feet. Farther into the trees, where the protection from the wind is greater, the stumps are from six to eight feet high.[27]

A short distance downstream from this camp is an outcropping of rocks. Charles Elliott and Frank Spencer both referred to seeing inscriptions on rocks in this area--specifically recalled were a V, perhaps for Vinsonhaler, and an upside-down U or horseshoe. While these markings have not been relocated, a well-weathered, broken ax handle was discovered deeply buried in the grass at the edge of these rocks. Heavy usage of upper Wannamaker Creek by sheep-herders and hunters makes it difficult to determine exactly what artifacts belonged to the Frémont expedition and which, though old, may have been left by later intruders.[28] The herders of the Wannamaker drainage were not of the same family as those who grazed the southern slopes of Mesa Mountain. They may not have had the same knowledge of nor respect for the expedition as those who had accompanied Alexis Godey on his rescue mission in the winter of 1849.

FS Trail 787 to the northwest across Palmer Mesa would be the route pursued by Charles Preuss's party in the attempt to find a way off the mountain. This trail and FS Trail 784 can be followed across the Continental Divide onto tributaries of Cochetopa Creek, but the area northwest of Halfmoon Pass is very rugged. The Trujillo Creek stumps are located in Section 30, T42N, R3E. Four-wheel-drive Road 630 from the settlement of Agua Ramon can be used to reach Trujillo Creek and the Wannamaker camp. It is a short hike from the ridge, where vehicular travel ends, to "Camp Dismal."

## CHRISTMAS CAMP

On Friday, December 22, after four days of trying to find a westward trail off the mountain, Frémont decided to move the expedition to the more protected southern slope of Mesa Mountain. In order to avoid total destruction, the men commenced dragging the baggage through the saddle that separates the waters of Wannamaker Creek from Rincon Creek, a tributary of Embargo Creek and the Rio Grande. The new camp, located at timberline on the west side of the creek, was three miles from "Camp Dismal."[29] Though it took several days to haul the baggage through the deep snow, Richard Kern mentioned that most of the supplies and equipment had been moved to the top of the hill by the end of the next day. Not until December 26, however, were the last of the packs brought into the new camp, where the Kerns and other members of the expedition had established their messes in six feet of snow.

"Camp Dismal" must have been dismal indeed when the Kern brothers returned to it for two loads on Christmas Day. The fire from John Scott's mess was smoldering; butchered mule carcasses lay in the snow; ravens circled overhead. A few surviving mules were seen wandering across the ridges above the camp.

The new site, or Christmas Camp, was called "Camp Hope" because Frémont had decided to dispatch a small rescue party to the New Mexican settlements to procure fresh pack animals and more supplies since only pork, macaroni, sugar, and mule meat were left. Charles Preuss stated that the plan was discussed carefully. Henry King, a veteran of Frémont's third expedition, would lead the rescue party. According to

Preuss, King was given $1,800 for supplies, but this money never was mentioned again. Estimating that the expedition was approximately one hundred miles from the Abiquiu settlements on the Chama River and that closer still were the settlements on the Rio Colorado north of Taos, the rescue party--King, Frederick Creutzfeldt, Thomas Breckenridge, and Bill Williams--agreed that by traveling day and night they would reach the New Mexican settlements in three or four days and be on their way back with relief by the time the rest of the men had moved the baggage off the mountain.

The most difficult part of the journey would be from this camp to the Rio Grande. Godey was to accompany the men that far. It seems strange that after all the problems the expedition had faced as a result of following Williams's suggestions, Frémont trusted him to be part of the rescue party, but no other member of the expedition had Williams's firsthand knowledge of the territory through which they were traveling.

After discussing the rescue plans, Frémont spent Christmas Day reading Blackstone's law while some of the men continued to move baggage from the top of the hill to the camp. To end what Richard Kern described as a "comfortable day," Alexis Godey prepared a Christmas feast. Years later Thomas Breckenridge recalled that they dined on baked mule, boiled mule, and several other kinds of mule, although this fanciful menu was not quoted in his original recollection, which appeared in the August 30, 1891, edition of the *Rocky Mountain News*. Actually, the men celebrated Christmas with a hearty meal of elk stew, minced-mulemeat pies, rice, doughnuts, biscuits, coffee, and a hot alcoholic beverage. Ben Kern became sick that night and spent the next several days recuperating.

On December 26 the rescue party started for the settlements. The rest of the men built sledges to facilitate moving the baggage to the next camp. Charles Preuss recorded that these did not work, so they were abandoned. Seventy-five years later Albert Pfeiffer, Jr., accidentally came across the remains of the sledges while deer hunting. In the 1950s the decaying debris of the sledges, wrapped in a baby blanket, was carried from the mountain by forest ranger Mark Ratliff and a group of San Luis Valley citizens. The sledge runners-- pieces of evidence that definitely confirm the location of a Frémont camp--are now on display at the Rio Grande County Museum in Del Norte, Colorado.[30]

Many have wondered why Frémont's men did not make snowshoes to help them conquer the deep drifts. Preuss, who made the only mention of snowshoes, stated that no materials were available for their construction. With the branches of trees and willows and the hides of dead mules, it would seem that some kind of shoe could have been designed to facilitate the journey through the snow. Perhaps the men were so confident the rescue party would be successful that they did not feel the need to exert the extra effort necessary to manufacture snowshoes. This was the reason cited by Preuss for leaving behind the mule meat--too "troublesome" to bother.

The view from the 12,000-foot ridges of Mesa Mountain allows an easy reconnaissance of the drainage patterns of the many streams that head on the mountain and flow toward the floor of the San Luis Valley. The ascent into the La Garita Mountains had been from the east. McGehee wrote in his manuscript, "The Colonel determined to endeavor as quickly as possible to return by a different direction to the Rio Grande." The initial attempt to descend from the heights where the expedition met with defeat was to the south along Rincon and Embargo creeks.

By December 27 the expedition had started to move toward a camp on Rincon Creek. Bundles of equipment were shot down the steep slope or ridden like giant inner tubes. Since Ben Kern was feeling weak, the other messes helped the Kern brothers transport their baggage to the new camp. According to Preuss, a few animals were alive but it was impossible to drive them through the snow. Entries in the Kerns' diaries describe the days as fine, warm, beautiful, sunny, pleasant, and the men as glib. Birds were singing. Morale was good.

Relief was expected within a week, and there were enough provisions to carry the men beyond that time. Meals consisted of mule and cornmeal or mule soup and coffee. On December 29, Ben Kern mentioned that his Indian mule was butchered since it was the fattest of those still alive.

Having transferred much of the baggage to the new camp in the canyon below the Christmas Camp, the men, filled with hope three days earlier, now faced disappointment. Alexis Godey, returning from the Rio Grande, announced that steep cliffs downstream prohibited moving the baggage along the same route used by the rescue party. Ben Kern wrote in his diary that Godey returned with the message that it was too steep to save the baggage and "we will have to retrace our steps back up a hard road & take another trail."

For three days the men dragged the heavy packs uphill toward Mesa Mountain and a route of retreat that, according to Thomas Martin, Frémont had seen during the ascent--the open parks of Groundhog and La Garita creeks. Micajah McGehee also stated that the main party was unable to follow the trail of the rescue party and had to find another route to the floor of the San Luis Valley.[31] On December 30 Ben Kern wrote that "Camp Disappointment" would be behind the expedition as soon as the bedding was moved.

There is no Forest Service trail from "Camp Dismal" on Wannamaker Creek to "Camp Hope"; therefore, it is difficult to locate the Christmas Camp from that direction. "Camp Hope" can be located by backtracking to the northeast along FS Trail 787, then turning to the southeast toward Section 28, T42N, R3E, and passing through the willows on the ridge that separates Rincon Creek from an unnamed tributary to the west. In the brush-filled expanses between fingers of forest is a post marking FS Trail 885. This trail leads east toward Rincon Creek and ends at the edge of the forest where forest ranger E. S. Ericson placed a sign identifying the Christmas Camp. Among the trees are the stumps left by the several messes of the fourth expedition. Between the Wannamaker camp and the Christmas Camp, in Section 29, T42N, R3E, lies a copse of trees with stumps characteristic of other Frémont camps. Forest Service personnel and the author agree that though there is no mention of this camp in the diaries, it matches other Frémont sites and probably was used as a rest area as the men moved across the ridge between the two main camps.

It is possible to reach the Christmas Camp by following FS Road 640 from the Cathedral Creek campground. In Section 33, just beyond the private property within the Rio Grande National Forest, Trail 885 leaves a logging road designated as 4x4 Road 791 and proceeds northwest through heavy forest. This trail, though marked with blazes, is difficult to follow because a mountain cyclone in the mid-1970s scattered trees like pickup sticks. After leaving the timber, the trail crosses the unnamed west fork of Rincon Creek, continues up the ridge separating the two creeks, and after passing the trail-marker described above, winds through the brush toward the Christmas Camp. This last section is the same trail intercepted by traveling southeast from the Wannamaker camp.

The only Frémont camp that has not been located in the San Juan Mountains is "Camp Disappointment." The camp should be in the canyon downstream from the Christmas Camp. Heavy timber growth in this area has hampered the search for this site, which possibly is the place Myers Creek rancher Charles Keck once saw a shovel with a branch growing through it high in an aspen tree. His son, Carl Keck, recalls that in 1941, while moving cattle off Mesa Mountain, the Kecks passed a rock ledge littered with brass rings and buckles. Two logs resembling the runners of a sledge lay among the trees, which were a mixture of aspen and bristlecone pine. In the crotch of a high stump, Carl Keck found a McClellan packsaddle complete with strapping. He left the saddle, intending to retrieve it later, but World War II changed his plan. The litter at the site suggested that the sledge may have plummeted down the steep slope, dumping some of the baggage among the trees.

After leaving "Camp Disappointment," the expedition worked its way toward the ridge that divides Rincon Creek from West Embargo Creek. Mule bones have been found scattered across this ridge.

## EMBARGO CREEK

On New Year's Eve, the Kerns' mess settled into a new camp in an open canyon with thick pines and willows growing along a wildly flowing creek. Ben Kern described large perpendicular rock walls, and Richard Kern noted copper-

colored rocks. This is an apt description of East Embargo
Creek. The willows jut into the forest like fingers. A great
copper-colored cliff of Fish Canyon tuff rises above the timber.
Beneath that cliff, in a small, detached grove of trees on the
west side of the creek, so typical of all Frémont camps, are a
few stumps. These stumps are not as high as stumps in other
camps, but Ben Kern noted that the snow here was only two
feet deep. There are not as many stumps as in other sites, but
again the Kern brothers' entries reveal that their mess was
the only one camped here. The other men were three miles
ahead. Ben referred to a "novel loneliness" as he, his brothers, Andrew Cathcart, and the two Indians sang and "made
merry." While Ned Kern prepared mule for the New Year's
Day treat of minced pies, Richard read and wrote later that
they "fired out the old year and passed the pleasantest night"
since their start. In his watercolor dated December 31, 1848,
Richard Kern depicted copper-colored cliffs rising above the
dark evergreen forest (Amon Carter collection).

The New Year's Eve camp can be located by retracing FS Trail 787,
which leads from Rincon Creek to the northeast toward the headwaters of East Embargo Creek. FS Trail 787 intersects with Embargo Creek Trail 792. The camp is located near the line between
Section 22 and Section 15, T42N, R3E, in a small copse of trees just
a few hundred feet west of where Trail 792, marked by a pile of
copper-colored rocks, crosses East Embargo Creek. Just as Ben Kern
described it, this camp lies below a massive perpendicular rock
wall. Downstream from the camp are thick growths of willows and
several beaver ponds. Embargo Creek can be an extremely hostile
environment in the summer months. Electrical storms develop quickly
above the ridges at its head and seem to be channeled along its
course as though attracted by the rock outcroppings. Extreme caution
should be used when hiking through this area. Better camping sites
can be found on other streams.

## THE GROUNDHOG CREEK CAMPS
The New Year's Eve camp of the Kerns' mess was separated
from the campsite of the other members of the expedition,
who were approximately three miles to the east at the head

of Groundhog Creek. McGehee wrote, "We would move camp three or four miles at a time." The Groundhog Creek camp, which later was to become the Kerns' haven while they waited for the rescue party to arrive and relieve them from the toil of moving the baggage off the mountain, was occupied longer than any other campsite. From this camp the other messes began working their way toward the floor of the San Luis Valley by following the drainage of Groundhog Creek through its wide park to the confluence with La Garita Creek.

Another camp was established about three miles downstream from the upper Groundhog Creek camp, which by now was occupied by the Kern brothers. From this second camp Lorenzo Vinsonhaler and the other men moved back and forth along the stream as they dragged the heavy bundles toward a cache where the baggage was to be left until the rescue party returned with fresh animals. This cache, established several miles farther down La Garita Creek nearer the floor of the San Luis Valley and identified by a large rock outcropping, was known as the "Colonel's camp."

Ben Kern's notes reflect the depression that affected the Kern brothers for several days. Scientific specimens collected for friends and academies of science and the Kerns' personal belongings were consolidated into a tremendous bale that was moved with great effort to the Groundhog Creek camp. Ben wrote that he was able to let the bedding, packed in parfleches, and other baggage slide downhill as he moved it toward the Vinsonhaler camp, but he had to crawl on his elbows and knees to return to the upper camp.

The Kerns spent the night of January 1, 1849, in the Groundhog Creek camp and did not abandon it until January 11, the day King's relief party was expected to arrive. Richard erected a crude shelter on January 2 and spent the night alone in a "hermit's camp" at the head of Groundhog Creek while his brothers returned to the New Year's Eve camp to burn books and discard the least valuable of their personal belongings. According to Ben, Richard's simple shelter was rebuilt to prepare for an approaching storm--"good shanty finished for the storm."

On January 3 Ben Kern described the mental and physical conditions of some of the men. He stated that he was "weak & dispirited" and that he had given out a quarter mile from camp. "Weak, melancholy" referred to Raphael Proue, who came by the Kerns' camp long after dark. After cheering brother Ned by saying all would be fine, Ben noted that he had eyed some mice hungrily and had wished for a mousetrap. This was a strange comment since just two days earlier the Kerns had shared a New Year's Eve feast of mule meat, buffalo, buffalo fat, meat pies, soup, and coffee. By January 4 they were supping on fat pork and macaroni. These diary entries make it difficult to believe that Ben Kern and his brother had reached a stage of hunger sufficient to cause them to cast a "hungry eye" at mice.

By this time Frémont's mess had reached the "river" or the bottomlands of the San Luis Valley. Alexis Godey and Charles Preuss returned to the upper camps to supervise the continuing removal of the baggage. Preuss stopped to build a fire in the Kerns' camp while Ben Kern spent the day sewing as "men passed on with loads." Here may be noted fuel for the animosity that some members of the expedition felt toward the Kern brothers--feelings that surfaced after Frémont departed for the New Mexican settlements and left the expedition under the command of Lorenzo Vinsonhaler. One can imagine the dismay of fatigued, hard-working men as they shared their labor and food (George Hubbard supplied the Kerns' mess with goat meat on the sixth) with these Philadelphia gentlemen, who in their naïveté rested, played the flute, read, and waited for news from below. This period of rest actually may have saved the members of the Kerns' mess since modern wilderness survival techniques emphasize conserving energy, but the extra stress placed upon the other members of the expedition also may have contributed to their exhaustion and inability to survive.

The upper Groundhog Creek camp with its numerous stumps, hacked or cut on the diagonal, is at timberline on the west bank of the stream in a grove of trees detached from the main forest. The stumps are not as high as in previous camps, but Thomas Martin recalled that the route off the mountain lay through a valley with considerably less snow. Frank Spencer marked this camp on a map after he visited Mesa Mountain with Albert Pfeiffer, Jr. Frank White, a descendant of La Garita sheepherders, also referred to a camp at the head of El Rito de Bole Alto (Groundhog Creek), which the herders avoided because it had belonged to the expedition. Lying between the stumps and the creek in an open, flat, grassy area is the right-angled outline of the structure that was Richard Kern's "good shanty."[32]

The Groundhog Creek camp is reached by following FS Trail 792 up the ridge lying east of East Embargo Creek. Leaving this trail, which winds toward the summit of Mesa Mountain, Frémont's route would lie due east across this ridge, which separates Embargo and Groundhog creeks. An unofficial trail with no markings skirts a mountain tarn that contains water most of the summer. The stumps of the Groundhog Creek camp, which lies in the northwest corner of Section 23, T42N, R3E, near the line between Section 23 and Section 14, T42N, R3E, can be seen among the trees as soon as the ridge into the Groundhog Creek drainage is passed.

The next camp on Groundhog Creek was an overnight camp occupied on January 6 by some of the men who were helping to move baggage toward the La Garita camps. FS Trail 794 follows to the southeast along the east bank of Groundhog Creek through Section 23 for approximately one mile. At the point where Groundhog Park begins to widen in Section 24 and the clearly marked trail emerges from the forest and passes through the grasses and marshes of a slough, stands a massive rock outcropping with many protected crannies along its south side. In two of these shelters, under six inches of debris, bits of charcoal from campfires were discovered in 1976.

Lorenzo Vinsonhaler's camp was three miles from the upper Groundhog Creek camp--approximately the distance from the headwaters of Groundhog Creek to its confluence with La Garita Creek. After flowing southeast through its expansive park, Groundhog Creek makes a great bend to the north in Section 30, T42N, R4E, passes between a short span of canyon walls, emerges into La Garita Park, and joins with La Garita Creek. FS Trail 794 from

Groundhog Park connects with FS Trail 793 in Section 17. Stumps are located here on the south-facing slope, but they are neither as extensive nor as concentrated as in the upper Groundhog Creek camp. These stumps may mark one of the several resting places used by the men as they worked the baggage from the mountain toward the cache. The Groundhog Creek camps can be reached by taking FS Road 650 from Embargo Creek to Groundhog Park and intercepting the trails to the camps.

## THE CAVE AND "POINT OF ROCKS"

On January 11 the Kerns' mess finally left the upper Groundhog Creek camp to meet the anticipated relief party. Richard Kern's entry--"Moved towards Cols camp [and] left early . . . to meet and hurry the mules"--seems to reflect his lack of understanding of the seriousness of the situation. Proceeding toward the river, Richard Kern and Andrew Cathcart met Micajah McGehee and Elijah Andrews. Kern recorded that this small party camped "under the shelving rock below a cave" and spent a comfortable night though their supper was boiled parfleche and their breakfast was the rawhide rope used to tow the baggage. McGehee's description of this encounter and the cave is more detailed:

> Between the last camps over a bleak and barren stretch of seven miles before reaching the river, the cold was unusually severe and perfectly unbearable . . . One day I started across this stretch, determined to go on to the river that night or freeze. Andrews started with me but, before we could get half way across, he became exhausted and lay down upon the snow, declaring that he could go no further . . . I could not leave him; so, proceeding a short distance, I got him into a cave of the rock, which afforded a shelter against the severity of the storm.

McGehee climbed to the top of the hill and rolled down piñon for a fire. "By this time, two others, Capt. Cathcart and R. Kern, arrived to take shelter from the storm. They had not a thing to eat, and we had our last portion." The day before each man had been given "a cupful of boiled macaroni and a cup of sugar." McGehee and Andrews were warming their portions, which they offered to share, when "the last mouthful that we had to eat on earth" was upset into the fire. McGehee stated that they stayed in the cave for two days while other members of the expedition took shelter among the rocks below. Someone who had stopped previously at the cave had left behind some rawhide snowshoe string, which McGehee and his comrades cooked into a glue and mixed with the pulverized bones of a wolf's carcass--"upon this mess, we four lived for two days."

While McGehee and Richard Kern differed slightly in their accounts of the trek to the "Colonel's camp," both men revealed the beginning of the dissolution of the expedition. No longer were the members banded together into supportive messes. Instead, they were working toward salvation by twos and threes. Ben Kern, John Stepperfeldt, and Carver were camped a short distance downstream from the cave among some willows.

---

Located halfway up the south-facing slope above La Garita Creek, the cave in which the four hungry, haggard wanderers sought refuge is directly across from the La Garita Cow Camp, which is private property within the Rio Grande National Forest. FS Trail 793 leads to a short length of very rough 4x4 road that passes through this property. McGehee's description of the wind, which was so fierce he would "have to lie flat down, at times, to keep from being swept off," is appropriate for La Garita Canyon. On a day that seems calm elsewhere in the San Luis Valley, zephyrs whistle along this stream as though being siphoned through a wind tunnel.

The baggage, which had been dragged along the creek bottoms in seventy-pound bundles, was being cached near a site known among Frémont's men as "point of rocks." Quite possibly Frémont hoped to continue to California via Cochetopa Pass after acquiring more supplies and pack animals; thus, the men attempted to save as much of the baggage as possible and to store it where it could be retrieved easily.

The term "point of rocks" is not uncommon in the San Luis Valley. Since most of the creeks heading in the San Juan Mountains have distinctive rock outcroppings, pinpointing the exact location of the cache was not easy. The early settlers at Del Norte had their "point of rocks," located behind the Rio Grande County Courthouse, as did settlers along San Francisco Creek, Pinos Creek, the Saguache River, and several other streams. Most of these outcroppings are not visible from the floor of the San Luis Valley; others do not fit the criteria for the route of the fourth expedition. The "point of rocks" marking the baggage cache had to be distinctive and easily recognizable--a landmark. Since the days of the first Spanish excursions into the valley of the Rio del Norte, one massive rock, jutting above the low hills along the west side of the valley, has borne a name reflective of its shape: the sentry box of a fortress--*la garita*-- a landmark located easily from the floor of the San Luis Valley.

Logic dictates that Frémont's cache would have been near this easily identifiable formation; however, final evidence was not available until 1984, when historian David Weber visited Fred Cron, Jr., in Pennsylvania. Among the watercolors that had been stored in the basement of the old hotel at Dingman's Ferry was one titled *Point of Rocks*. This watercolor shows a formation of cliffs bordering a narrow valley with low willows growing along the banks of a stream--a picture that would have been similar to rock outcroppings along several streams. Light and shadow indicate that the formation in the watercolor faces south or west, which narrows the possibilities of its location. The decisive factor for determining the exact location of Frémont's "point of rocks" is the background in Kern's watercolor--a heavily forested, dark blue, twin-peaked mountain.

On a cold Saturday morning in early January 1984, Barbara Colville of Del Norte, Colorado, and the author snapped on cross-country skis and broke trail through the two and a half feet of snow that covered FS Road 670 along La Garita Creek. Approximately a mile upstream from the La Garita formation with its massive stone face thrust toward the sky, south-facing volcanic cliffs fifteen to twenty feet high border the creek and create an extensive solar wall, which keeps the ground between the cliffs and the creek's north bank barren of snow. Along the creek are thickets of willow, exactly as in Richard Kern's watercolor. The view westward from this rock wall is of a twin-peaked mountain so heavily forested that its color designates its name--Blue Mountain.

A few years earlier, the author, using only the descriptions and mileages recorded by members of the expedition, selected an extension of this same rock wall as the possible site of the cache. From this lower location at the juncture of Little La Garita and La Garita creeks, the distinctive Blue Mountain is blocked from view by a slight bend in the creek.

"Point of Rocks" lies within state land in Section 36, T42N, R5E. Those following Frémont's trail should remember that federal and state laws prohibit prospecting for or removal of artifacts without specific permission from the appropriate government agencies. Treasure hunters need to recall that the New Mexican settlers knew the exact location of Frémont's cache. Anything left behind would have been put to use by the end of the summer of 1849; anything overlooked would have been salvaged by the La Garita herders and their families.[33]

## THE RESCUE PARTIES

Disaster struck the fourth expedition on January 9. Raphael Proue, an aged veteran of all of Frémont's expeditions and a loyal follower who had labored to move the baggage from camp to camp, lay in the snow dying, as Preuss recorded, from "cold and exhaustion, [or] some other illness." One wonders if the ordeal on the mountain had turned the men's hearts as cold as the wind. Richard Kern stated that Vinsonhaler had found Proue with his legs frozen and had wrapped blankets around the dying man, but it appears that no one made an effort to move Proue to a camp, to fill him with hot liquid, to revive him. McGehee recounted, "We passed and repassed his lifeless body, not daring to stop long enough in this intense cold to perform the useless rites of burial."

Apparently this tragedy convinced Frémont that if he personally did not start for the New Mexican settlements, the entire expedition would meet with Proue's fate. On January 11, having waited eighteen days for King's return and convinced that only Indians could have kept the rescue party from its goal, Frémont with Alexis Godey, Charles Preuss, fourteen-year-old Theodore McNabb, and Jackson Saunders left the rest of the men, according to Preuss, with orders to "finish transporting the baggage to the river, to store it there in the lodge, and then to follow us." McGehee wrote: "Taking just enough provision before it was all exhausted to do them down the river"--a one-day supply of food--Frémont's small party, with bedding tied to their backs, started toward the

New Mexican settlements. Preuss recounted that they soon found horse tracks assumed to be King's messenger and cursed as they thought he had turned back. An Indian camp near King's made them "apprehensive [that] . . . King's party [might have been] attacked!"

The first rescue party was not far ahead of Frémont. After descending Rincon Creek into Embargo Creek's valley, Henry King's party had worked its way along the Rio Grande toward the New Mexican settlements. Campfires revealed to Frémont's mess that once on the plain east of the gap of the Rio Grande, the four men, so sure of success at "Camp Hope," had soon lost their zeal. Four to five days had been used to cover short distances of ten or eleven miles. Charles Taplin stated later that King's diary revealed Williams had delayed the rescue party. Thomas Breckenridge also recalled that it was Williams who urged the men to leave the protection of the river by claiming he had seen the smoke of Indians who were after his scalp. Once exposed to the full fury of the winter winds that whip across the sagebrush-covered flats south of present Monte Vista, Colorado, the members of the rescue party found themselves struggling for their own survival. Fingers and feet were frozen, and bones protruded from bare flesh. Eyes, blinded by the highly reflective field of white surrounding the men, became inflamed and swollen.

Within fifteen days after leaving "Camp Hope," the original rescue party had exhausted all provisions, including those procured en route--a crow, a small mountain sheep, and an otter, which Thomas Breckenridge claimed he still could taste after forty-three years. Eventually everything made of leather was consumed in an attempt to relieve starvation. Having had nothing to eat for eight days, the men became delirious. King fell behind. In 1891 Breckenridge, residing near Telluride, Colorado, reminisced about King's death:

> It was at this stage of things that we lost King. This was a little above where Alamosa, Colo., now stands. With great difficulty

he had been forcing his way through the snow. He was freezing and starving and was becoming fainter and fainter. He was trying hard to hold his courage and strength. He stopped to rest more frequently, till finally he told us to go on a piece and build a fire and he would rest awhile and then follow. We went on a short distance and there started a fire. But King did not come.

Ignoring Williams, who insisted that King must be dead because a raven--great, black scavenger of the San Luis Valley-- had been circling overhead, Frederick Creutzfeldt went back to help his comrade into camp. According to Breckenridge, Creutzfeldt returned alone, so despondent he became demented. The next morning Williams, saying he would stay with the exhausted Creutzfeldt, urged Breckenridge to go ahead. Breckenridge recalled that after leaving his friends, he came over a ridge and saw a deer along the bank of a stream: "It was with a kind of nervous despair I raised my rifle. I could hardly see owing to the terrible condition of my snowblind and inflamed eyes. But I felt that I could not miss my aim, for it was life or death. The deer leaped into the air and fell dead and we were saved." For years Breckenridge's story was discounted as fantasy until the discovery of Charles Preuss's diary, which revealed that the surviving three members of the rescue party were devouring deer meat when Frémont came upon them near the San Luis Hills.

Breckenridge's account continued: "At that time . . . we seemed hardly like human beings, we were so near dead from hunger, cold and exposure. When I killed that deer we were so near starved that we ate both entrails and flesh."[34] Frémont wrote to his wife Jessie that these three wild, emaciated men were "the most miserable objects I have ever seen." The horrors associated with King's death had occurred on January 12 or 13--a few days after Frémont had left his camp on the La Garita.

The original rescue party had to have spent at least two days reaching the Rio Grande. According to Breckenridge they had descended by way of Embargo Creek, but it is impossible to pinpoint their campsites. The men would have spent one night where Embargo (Myers) Creek flows into the Rio Grande. Alexis Godey then started back to rejoin the main party and advised them that they could not move the baggage along the same route. Four days had passed during Godey's absence from the main party.

The rescue party never covered the mileage anticipated, as fatigue from fighting the harsh cold reduced travel to three or four miles per day. Somewhere between the present towns of Monte Vista and Alamosa, Colorado, they left the Rio Grande and cut diagonally across the open prairie. Here, away from the protection of the timber, the virtually constant southwest winds create an extreme chill factor and cause snow to drift. The rescue party had moved as far as the San Luis Hills when Breckenridge killed the deer. Frémont found the three emaciated survivors near Pike's Stockade at the confluence of the Rio Grande and the Conejos River.

---

There is no official Forest Service trail following directly along upper Rincon Creek, but FS Trail 885 and 4x4 Road 791, described previously, lead from the Christmas Camp to Cathedral campground and Road 640, a branch of Embargo Creek Road 650. From Elkhorn Ranch either the dirt road along the north side of the river or U.S. Highway 160 along the south side of the Rio Grande will follow approximately the route of the rescue party as they moved east toward the floor of the San Luis Valley.[35]

An impression of the rescue party's route after leaving the Rio Grande is obtained by following U.S. Highway 160 from Del Norte east to the Alamosa County Line Road, then zigzagging south to Colorado Highway 368, east to U.S. Highway 285, south again to La Jara and Colorado Highway 126, and then east toward Sanford and the San Luis Hills.

The day after Frémont and his companions saw horse tracks and assumed that King may have sent a messenger, the second relief party came across an Indian with whom they were able to converse in Spanish.[36] Having used their meager provisions sparingly, this group had been without food but one day. The Indian led the men to his lodging and in the morning fed them corn mush, venison, and coffee. With gifts and promises of a reward, Frémont convinced the Indian to lead his party to the settlements on the Rio Colorado. Preuss mentioned that the Indian provided four poor horses to ride, which allowed the exhausted men to regain their energies. As this group proceeded along the river toward a grove of trees, they noticed smoke. Crouched around a fire "devouring dried deer meat" were the three surviving members of the original relief party. The second rescue party, having traveled four days, had intercepted the first rescue party twenty-two days after the men left "Camp Hope" approximately fifty miles away.

Placing the three "skinny and hollow-eyed" survivors upon the horses, Frémont continued toward the Rio Colorado settlements rather than Abiquiu, which he decided was too distant if the rest of the expedition were to be saved.[37] After leaving the meandering Rio Grande above La Sauses Gorge (correct Spanish would be Los Sauces) and crossing the riblike hills of the Costilla Plain--undoubtedly following the Kiowa Trail, which still is used ceremonially by the Pueblo Indians--Frémont and his companions arrived at the settlements near present Questa, New Mexico. Flour and goats were available here, but Alexis Godey had to continue to the settlement of Arroyo Hondo to get mules to transport the supplies to the men left in the San Luis Valley. Finally, relief was on the way.

## THE RELIEF CAMPS

Although Frémont had left instructions that the other members of the expedition were to follow the same day he left, it was not until January 16, the day the two rescue parties met, that the men finally finished moving the baggage and began their exodus from the mountains. Lorenzo Vinsonhaler, waiting at the cache and tired of delays, had sent word to the Kerns' mess that the Colonel expected the men to "hasten on down as speedily as possible to the Mouth of Rabbit River," where they would meet a relief party, and that they had better hurry if they wished to accompany Frémont to California by the southern route.

The choice of the Conejos or Rabbit River for a rendezvous was appropriate since Frémont knew about Zebulon Pike's construction of a stockade at the mouth of the Conejos in January 1807. If standing, it would provide shelter for the men. Frémont also may have known of the existence of summer settlements along the Conejos River.[38] These, too, would have provided shelter and the possibility of food, in the form of stored seeds, if the men were able to locate any of these simple farming communities. Surely the easily recognizable Conejos River, clearly indicated on both the Miera y Pacheco map and Zebulon Pike's crude sketch as the Rio Grande's major east-flowing tributary, was the best place Frémont could have directed his men to wait for relief.

On January 16, 1849, thirty-eight days after passing Hell Gate, the members of the fourth expedition emerged from the San Juan Mountains. Thomas Martin recalled, "In going down the other side [than the route taken by the rescue party] it took us 16 days to go as many miles." Richard Kern's notation that his camp two miles below the "big rock" where the baggage had been cached was near the "old Elk camp" provides further confirmation that the expedition had descended by way of La Garita Creek--its gap less than three miles from the Carnero Creek camp where Godey had killed two elk before the ascent into the mountains.

The effect of the delays by the Kerns' mess soon became evident. The Indian Manuel, his feet frozen, begged to be shot, but he returned to a lodge near the cache after his pleas were refused. Though he lived and later was rescued by Godey, the first survivors to reach Frémont reported that Manuel had perished.

The next day the men moved six miles farther along the frozen La Garita Creek into that area known as "the bottoms" and waited while John Scott attempted to hunt. McGehee reported that Henry Wise, who was ten miles below the camp, "lay down upon the ice on the river and died." Toward evening Carver, claiming that he had a plan for salvation, urged his comrades to return to the mountains with him. Fearful for their own safety, Carver's companions allowed him to wander from camp. Carver found Manuel in the lodge and then headed upstream toward the cache. Since there was no further mention of Carver or his corpse, he was counted among the victims; however, Preuss's reference to Indians having seen a man walking across the floor of the valley with two human legs across his back, a story Preuss was inclined to believe, adds a possibility of intrigue to Carver's disappearance.

Only a mile and a half were passed the following day, but Richard Kern stated that more delays were necessary to give the unsuccessful hunters a chance to procure some food. Finally, the men reached the river "near where we first struck"-- the plains area west-northwest of the sand dunes where La Garita and Carnero creeks joined the Saguache. Mileages in Richard's diary reveal that this spot was fifty-five miles from the place where Godey would meet the first group of survivors.

In this camp, the members openly began quarreling among themselves. By the time the slow-moving Kerns' mess reached the camp, Vinsonhaler's mess had consumed most of a deer that had been killed. Richard Kern complained bitterly that ten men had received only two shoulder blades for their share though other sources suggest that the portion may have been the front quarters. After thoroughly denouncing Vinsonhaler-- "man left in charge was totally unfit, on account of want of tact and experience and correct principles"--Richard recorded his belief that Vinsonhaler intended to take the deer and strong men and push for Abiquiu, leaving "the rest of us to perish." Thomas Martin's account confirms that he had urged Vinsonhaler to allow the stronger men to hasten down the river without waiting for the others to ensure that someone would reach a settlement and send relief.

As the men continued another three miles toward the south, all signs of game disappeared. Temperatures often plummet to thirty degrees below zero in the lowest elevations of the central plain of the San Luis Valley. There was less snow on the ground, but the men were too weakened to really appreciate this boon. The formidable, jagged peaks of Tres Tetones dominated the eastern skyline. The Indians, Juan and Gregorio, claiming a threat had been made to kill and eat them if the situation became worse, left the Kerns' mess.

January 21 was the last day for the old companions Antoine Morin and Vincent Tabeau (Sorrel), who had pushed ahead and reached the Rio Grande before the others. The sixteen-mile march, which almost "used up" the weaker members, according to Richard Kern, placed the men about four miles above the oxbow of the great river. Again Martin and John Scott argued that all would perish if the stronger members did not strike out on their own and drive as quickly as possible toward the New Mexican settlements. This time Vinsonhaler succumbed to their demands and gave up command, an act of "rascality almost without parallel," in Kern's eyes. The stronger men agreed that any man who could not maintain the pace would be left behind with a fire for comfort while his companions hastened downriver to secure relief or hurry a returning rescue party. This same day, January 22, Alexis Godey, after returning to Rio Colorado with thirty mules, had gathered bread, meat, and drivers for the lifesaving *entrada* back into the San Luis Valley.

Micajah McGehee's narrative divided the men into three groups after the dissolution of the expedition with Josiah Ferguson and Benjamin Beadle staying together. Richard Kern and Thomas Martin placed the men in two groups--the stronger and the weaker. The three Kern brothers, Elijah Andrews, McGehee, John Stepperfeldt, and Andrew Cathcart were in the group left behind. Henry Rohrer started with the stronger men but soon fell behind and joined the Kerns' camp. One member of the expedition deserving citation was Charles Taplin. Though strong enough to continue downstream with his companions, he chose to stay with the weaker men to serve as hunter and guide in hopes that they would survive until relief arrived.

According to Thomas Martin, the stronger men, traveling day and night, made their way toward the mouth of the Conejos River; however, the other men, described by Richard Kern as "too weak to move," advanced only four miles downstream. Here, after promising not to leave anyone who still lived, they waited for relief or the end of their ordeal. Bugs, a wolf carcass--"hair and all"--and two prairie chickens, including the pinfeathers, were used to sustain life.

Ben Kern did not make an entry in his diary after January 6, 1849, when he sat dejectedly in the upper Groundhog Creek camp, and Richard Kern's last entry, until after being rescued by Godey, was January 23; therefore, the sole description of the relief camp and the events that occurred before Godey's arrival comes from Micajah McGehee. As McGehee, Stepperfeldt, and Taplin were sitting by the fire, one of the other members of the group came forward with a proposal that they use the corpses of Andrews and Rohrer to stay alive until help arrived. McGehee, urging that they wait at least three days, stated, "After finding that we cannot possibly bear up longer, there will then be time enough to think of adopting so horrible alternative."

Two days later, as the men "sat in the deepest gloom," Taplin thought he heard a call. "Hush! said one, and we all listened intently." Riding toward them was Alexis Godey, whom they mistook to be Frémont until he arrived at the camp. While drinking a nutritious porridge of blue cornmeal, called *atole*, the Kerns and their companions learned that many of those who had pushed ahead had expended their strength and had died. With the exception of Taplin and Edward Kern, the Kerns' mess was composed of greenhorns, men who had never faced the hardships of the wilderness before; yet, most of these men survived while many of their more experienced comrades perished.

According to Charles Preuss, it had taken Godey two days to find the survivors. The first evening he met the two Indians, who told him others followed. He fired a signal, and the next morning Lorenzo Vinsonhaler, Thomas Martin, and William Bacon met Godey near the spot where Frémont had discovered the original relief party about twenty miles downstream from the oxbow. These men had survived by killing a hawk and "prairie hens" and by eating part of a dead horse they had found. Upstream Godey and Vinsonhaler found John Scott, who had just built a fire. George Hubbard was two miles behind. One can imagine Godey's dismay upon finding Hubbard dead but still warm. Godey missed the Kerns' party but came upon Josiah Ferguson. His companion Beadle was dead. Ferguson, who knew that the Kern brothers and the others were downstream, accompanied Godey to their camp. Tears flowed as the starving explorers were reunited with their benefactor.

Leaving the men in camp with bread, cornmeal, and colts for meat, Godey and some of the New Mexicans continued to backtrack toward the cache. The bodies of Sorrel and Morin were found slumped together, comrades to the end. Upon reaching the lodge built in the camp at the "big rock," Godey found Manuel still alive. What touching scene occurred at this reunion was not recorded. Manuel reported that Carver, having killed a deer, had returned to the baggage cache. Godey and the New Mexicans tried to retrieve the baggage but abandoned their efforts when some of their animals perished from the cold. Only the lodge and its contents, including a trunk with some of Frémont's clothing and his instruments, were salvaged. The expedition's money and the latest in camp furniture, saddles, pack equipment, and clothes were left in the snows of the San Juan Mountains along with the mules' carcasses and the bodies of dead men.

---

As with the campsites of the relief parties, pinpointing the exact locations where the main party camped after leaving the mountains is impossible. The appearances of geographic features on the floor of the San Luis Valley have been altered by civilization: railroad beds, roads, plowed fields, stock ponds, canals, and buildings. Private land limits access to the area passed between the mountains and the reunions with Godey. The mileages given by Richard Kern and the ultimate destination, the New Mexican settlements, allow an approximate retracing by following public roads.

The route from the "big rock" camp, marked by the La Garita formation, would follow FS Road 670 until it leaves La Garita Canyon. From here the easiest modern route connects with Saguache County Road G, but several dirt roads also lead east across the old bottomlands of the La Garita drainage. The waters of both La Garita and Carnero creeks now are caught by the Rio Grande Canal, but in spring their subwaters continue to create marshes as far east as the Meadow Ranch on Saguache County Road 53.

After reaching the "Gunbarrel" Road (U.S. Highway 285), County Road G can be followed east for eight miles to Saguache County Road 53. This line, 37 degrees, 50 feet, in R9E, marks the approximate location of the camp where Thomas Martin first suggested dissolving the expedition after the men quarreled over the distribution of the deer that had been killed. Poorly maintained, dead-end dirt roads make the route from this camp to the Rio Grande even more difficult to follow. Saguache County Road 53, which becomes Road 6 after crossing Colorado Highway 112, would be in proximity. In dry weather a route following Road G to Saguache County Road 53, continuing south to Eight Mile Lane, then turning east to Twelve Mile Road and proceeding south onto the pavement, which zigzags toward Alamosa and crosses the Rio Grande by the State Bridge, would be closer to the route used by Frémont's men.

The Rio Grande of the early to middle 1800s would have been very different from the river today. Zebulon Pike described it as three miles wide at its oxbow, and Gwinn Harris Heap noted that many sloughs and quicksands made crossing the river treacherous. The old flood plain is now covered with housing developments, but the wild, wooded atmosphere still can be felt in a few places.

About four miles from where Vinsonhaler relinquished command, Godey found the Kern brothers and their companions in a camp just below the Rio Grande's great oxbow. This area can be reached by following State Street south through Alamosa to Twelfth Street, then continuing east. Just beyond East Avenue the road curves and becomes the South River Road. Approximately four tenths of a mile from this curve is a meadow where one can see Sierra Blanca through willows and cottonwoods, much as Richard Kern saw the massif when he sketched the "Relief Camp" in 1849.[39]

The Vinsonhaler mess had encountered Godey at the edge of the San Luis Hills about fifteen to twenty miles downstream from the Kerns' party. The South River Road continues east and south along section lines toward the old settlement of La Sauses and the area where Frémont found the first rescue party and Godey met the first survivors. In the 1870s a road followed this same line between Alamosa and La Sauses. The settlement of La Sauses, founded in 1863, lies west of a geologic formation known as La Sauses Gorge where the Rio Grande, almost in miniature of the magnificent Rio Grande Gorge, has channeled through the basalt formations in the area. The western skyline is dominated by Piedra Pintada and Bennett Peak marking the Summitville mining district in the Conejos Mountains.

## THE REUNION AT RIO COLORADO AND TAOS

One would think that the dispirited survivors, having been pushed to the limit, would have left the snowy expanses of the San Luis Valley and the site of their ordeals as quickly as possible, but a week passed before Vinsonhaler, Martin, and Bacon set out for the Rio Colorado settlements. The Kerns' mess, having joined Vinsonhaler and the other survivors in the lower camp, rested and recuperated another three days. Apparently the animosity between the two groups was not resolved as the stronger men started for the settlements the day after the Kern party arrived in camp.

In the meantime, Frémont had moved to Taos to be with his friend Kit Carson while Charles Preuss waited anxiously at Rio Colorado for Godey and the survivors. On February 6, 1849, fifteen days after Godey had departed from the settlements, Preuss greeted the first of his "hungry brothers," who arrived with tragic stories about the fates of their comrades. Having left before Godey's return from the cache, these men did not know that Manuel had been found alive; thus, the first information relayed to Frémont and recorded in a letter he was writing to his wife Jessie was that eleven members of the expedition had perished.

Godey finally rejoined the Kern party after the unsuccessful attempt to retrieve the baggage. The party crossed the Conejos River and began following Vinsonhaler and the others toward New Mexico. After traveling thirty-three miles, they overtook Julius Ducatel, the Indian Juan, and some of the New Mexicans, who were still in Vinsonhaler's last camp. A full stomach certainly had changed Richard Kern's outlook as now every day was a "fine day."

The men moved together to a camp on Culebra Creek ten miles away. Again they encountered deep snow with another six inches falling during the night. Richard Kern seemed to dawdle as the remnant of the expedition moved toward civilization. As he made his way toward Costilla Creek, fifteen miles from the Culebra camp, Richard almost became lost in a severe blizzard similar to those that often whip across the Costilla Plains even today. Kern accurately described the bottomland of the Costilla as "plenty [of] big timber." By the summer of 1849, the settlement of Costilla would be located along the banks of the creek. Today part of the community, known as Garcia, is in Colorado while the rest lies in New Mexico. Another fifteen miles of travel finally brought the men to the Rio Colorado settlements where they met Preuss and Frederick Creutzfeldt. Although Preuss lamented that all the baggage was lost, leaving him "poor as Job," he decided that having saved one's life was best.[40]

The next day the survivors started for "Rio Hondo" (Arroyo Hondo), but Richard Kern's horse soon "gave out" so Kern stayed overnight in the forest. Godey sent a man and a horse from the settlement. After Richard arrived at the village, he found his brother Ben, and they spent the night with William LeBlanc at Turley's mill.[41] The other men had continued to Taos in wagons.

On February 12, 1849, two full months after their ascent into the San Juan Mountains, Frémont, Charles Preuss, Alexis Godey, the Kern brothers, and the other sixteen survivors of the expedition were reunited in Taos. That same day Frémont, having decided who would continue with him to California by the lower Spanish Trail, or Gila route, left for Santa Fe and Albuquerque. Kit Carson's brother, Lindsey Carson, and Thomas Boggs, son of a former Missouri governor, had joined the expedition. Left in Taos were John Stepperfeldt, who was too weak to continue; the guide Bill Williams; Andrew Cathcart, for whose safety Preuss had been especially concerned; and Benjamin, Edward, and Richard Kern.[42]

By the mid-1860s, less than twenty years after Frémont's men had wandered through an uncivilized white wasteland, twenty-five settlements were strung along the Conejos and San Antonio rivers near their junctures with the Rio Grande. Travel between these settlements and the east side of the San Luis Valley passed along routes that utilized the natural fords of the Rio Grande.[43]

Although there were no official roads and few trails when Frémont and his men passed through the San Luis Valley, the early roads into and through the area would have followed the trails used by trappers, traders, and Indians just as surely as those foot travelers had followed the ancient game trails. Several maps of the San Luis Valley, made prior to and during the gold rush days in the San Juan Mountains, indicate the roads that had been developed to connect communities and geographic areas. By examining those first trails and roads, it is possible to determine Frémont's route to the New Mexican settlements.

The Kerns' party was camped on the west bank of the Rio Grande just below the oxbow when they were rescued by Godey. Vinsonhaler and the others were farther south, nearer the San Luis Hills. From these camps the men could have used the northern ford, or Conejos Ferry, to cross the Rio Grande, but Richard Kern recorded that they started toward the New Mexican settlements after crossing the Conejos River, which indicates that the survivors of the fourth expedition had followed the west bank of the Rio Grande southward from the "Relief Camp" to a good camp where Richard enjoyed several days of "eating colt's meat." Here Godey rejoined the men after his attempt to retrieve the baggage.

The camp on the Culebra (Snake) River was ten miles from this good camp. In the mid-1800s, a trail that forded the Rio Grande at the south end of La Sauses Gorge, just below the mouth of the Conejos River, cut diagonally to the southeast toward the Culebra River. The trail then joined the road, which followed the Culebra toward the old settlement of San Acacio, located four miles downstream from present San Luis.[44]

Today there is no road cutting diagonally from the San Luis Hills toward the Culebra settlements; therefore, modern travelers must continue south from La Sauses on the dirt road that joins with Colorado Highway 142 just west of the Rio Grande. Colorado Highway 142 connects Manassa, located near the first settlements on the Conejos, with San Luis and the Culebra villages. Ten miles east of the Rio Grande, the highway makes a double dog-legged jog so the road will pass through new San Acacio, which was built in 1910 as a terminus for the San Luis Valley Southern Railroad. At the southern corner of the double jog, a narrow, paved lane continues due east off Highway 142 to connect with Colorado Highway 159, eleven miles west of San Luis. Old San Acacio was located one mile west of this intersection. These three roads—Highway 142, the paved lane, and the eleven miles of Highway 159—are the old route between the Rio Grande and the Culebra settlements.

The old road connecting the Culebra villages with the New Mexican settlements skirted the west side of San Pedro Mesa, a part of the ancient floor of the San Luis Basin that has been thrust above the alluvial deposits. Colorado Highway 159 south follows closely the original road between old San Acacio and Costilla. After crossing the Costilla River (which still has "heavy timber"), the route that was used by the Indians, Spaniards, trappers, explorers, and eventually settlers to pass between the San Luis Valley and the settlements of northern New Mexico would have stayed close to the hillside for easy access to water and fuel and for protection against the elements. The Taos Plateau, forming the southern regions of the San Luis Basin, is a waterless, barren, windblown, hostile environment.[45]

The ancient north-south route through the southeastern region of the San Luis Valley was known locally as the Kiowa Trail, the Trapper's Trail, or Kit Carson's Trail. The original road, which often passes through private property, is not well maintained. Bad weather, rocks, and deep ruts make a vehicle with four-wheel-drive or high clearance essential for travel along any part of the old trace. Twice the road has been moved to the west so New Mexico Highway 522 is the modern version of the trail that for centuries carried travelers north or south along the base of the Sangre de Cristo Mountains. Although the modern highway is not the exact road used by Frémont, travelers retracing the fourth expedition's route to Taos will have a clear view of the terrain through which the men passed as they moved from Costilla through the Rio Colorado settlement of Questa to Arroyo Hondo and finally toward Taos. An occasional side trip into the Carson National Forest for a short walk or drive along the old road will give today's explorers a feeling for the area; however, they should be prepared for the unexpected—rain, snow, cold, sand, silt, mud, or water.

The original settlement of Rio Colorado, today's Questa, was east of the hill where New Mexico highways 522 and 38 intersect. The Kiowa Trail, which followed Cabresto Creek for a short distance, passed directly through the village. The trail crossed the Red River and continued along the ridges of several drainages. A rugged road typical of the original trail can be followed from Questa to San Cristobal. A dirt road, angling to the southeast approximately one mile south of the stoplight at the intersection of New Mexico highways 522 and 38, will lead to a bridge across the Red River. Turn right after crossing the river. The road then climbs a hill toward the commune of Lama. This road becomes FS Road 493, which leads to San Cristobal.

From San Cristobal south the original trace again becomes very rough and should be abandoned in favor of New Mexico 522 to Arroyo Hondo. Referred to as "Rio Hondo" by Frémont's men, the original settlement lies one mile east of the modern highway. New Mexico 150 east can be taken into the small village where not only Frémont's men but also George Ruxton a year earlier received warm food and lodging. The original trail came into the village past Turley's mill. A trace of that old road can be seen angling downhill at the site of the mill's ruins.

Dirt road 150 continues east toward the present settlement of Valdez. Just before reaching Valdez, one mile to the west of the hamlet, another dirt road swings south while 150 continues east into Valdez before making a right turn south and again becoming a paved road. Both roads follow the Arroyo Seco, but the dirt road, which passes private property, stays along the ridge above the arroyo, as did the original road, before rejoining with paved Highway 150 at the village of Arroyo Seco. Either road continues from here in a southerly direction to intersect with New Mexico 522, which proceeds southeast into Taos.

Several roads led from the north into the half dozen settlements known as Taos. Since none of the accounts mention the pueblo, the members of Frémont's expedition probably entered the small community of Taos along the same route as New Mexico 522 south of the blinking light, which marks the junctions of New Mexico highways 522 and 150 and U.S. Highway 64 from Tres Piedras. Instead of a broad, paved road, Frémont would have followed a narrow dirt lane to the home of his friend Kit Carson. Carson's home sat east of the plaza and today serves as a museum operated by the Kit Carson Foundation.

The original Taos plaza was much larger than the area bordered by modern businesses. The Blumenschein House and Harwood Foundation on Ledoux Street mark what was the southern edge of the plaza. The northern perimeter was about one half block south of Bent Street where both Charles and William Bent had homes. Padre Street was the western boundary.

The modern explorer, having retraced Frémont's route to Taos, where the Pathmarker, the survivors of the fourth expedition, and other individuals notable in western history passed moments of their lives, may wish to relax by visiting the many historical and cultural sites located in this colorful community before beginning some new adventure.[46]

## EPILOGUE

Although the research for this retracing of the route of John C. Frémont's fourth expedition has been extensive, many questions concerning the ill-fated expedition remain unanswered. Of primary interest is the exact location of "Camp Disappointment." Carl Keck's recollection of the debris scattered across the rock ledge and throughout the forest downstream from the Christmas Camp coincides with the location described by the Kern brothers and with Charles Preuss's statement that "a sled came to grief."

Unfortunately the opportunities for first-hand research diminish with each passing winter. The stumps, so long the standard for identifying the Frémont camps, are disintegrating or being destroyed by people who are either ignorant or uncaring. Forest Service archaeologist Vince Spero and his colleagues are attempting to record and preserve information about the sites while evidence is still available. With time, also, passes the opportunity to share the knowledge of the sheepherders, cattlemen, and other mountaineers, like George Ward, who moved across the expanses of Mesa Mountain during the late 1800s and early 1900s and who, like Bill Williams, knew the high country as well as the back of their own hands.

Yet, in spite of this inevitable passing of time, which takes Frémont's camps and trail toward obscurity, there are among each generation a few adventurers who are willing to lace their boots, strap on their packs, and trudge through the wilderness so that they can share a sense of destiny with John C. Frémont and the men of the fourth expedition.

1

**Prologue**

As San Luis Valley historian Ruth Marie Colville of Del Norte, Colorado, has commented, the men of Frémont's fourth expedition "constituted a strange mixture" including mountain men, a German mapmaker, French-Canadians, a blacksmith, a Scottish captain of the hussars, Philadelphia artists, a medical doctor, a freedman, a tubercular midshipman, three Indians, a Mississippi gentleman, and a teen-aged boy.

The narrative of Micajah McGehee provides the most complete roster of the men who accompanied Frémont into the mountains. Historians disagree as to spellings, but the names as cited in this work follow the definitive edition prepared by Mary Lee Spence, professor of history at the University of Illinois.

In the list that follows, the names of the ten who perished are preceded by a Maltese cross. Examination of the circumstances and characteristics of their deaths would indicate that they were victims of hypothermia. The subzero temperatures and persistent southwest winds of the San Luis Valley can make exposure hazardous even for modern hikers and hunters equipped with the protection of down jackets and insulated boots and mittens. One can but marvel at the levels of endurance exhibited by the men who accompanied explorers Zebulon M. Pike and John C. Frémont into the frigid, unexplored wilderness of the San Luis Valley.

The men who had been with Frémont previously were Thomas E. Breckenridge, Josiah Ferguson, Alexis Godey, Edward M. (Ned) Kern, ✠Henry King, Thomas Salathiel Martin, ✠Antoine Morin, ✠Raphael Proue, Charles Preuss, John Scott, ✠Vincent Tabeau (Sorrel), Charles Van Linneus Taplin, Lorenzo D. Vinsonhaler, William Sherley Williams, and three Indians brought from California in 1847--Gregorio, Juan, and Manuel. Traveling with Frémont for the first time were ✠Elijah T. Andrews, William Bacon, ✠Benjamin Beadle, Andrew Cathcart, ✠Carver,

Frederick Creutzfeldt, Julius E. Ducatel, ✠George Hubbard, Benjamin Kern, Richard H. Kern, Micajah McGehee, ✠Henry Rohrer, John S. Stepperfeldt, and ✠Henry J. Wise.

Two members of the expedition whose roles have been ignored by many writers were Jackson Saunders, a free servant from Senator Thomas Hart Benton's household, and Theodore McNabb, Alexis Godey's fourteen-year-old nephew.

James McDowell had left the expedition on October 27 at Westport, with a warning that fewer than half the men would reach California after much hardship. Amos Andrews, father of Elijah Andrews, started with the expedition but remained at Pueblo. Another member, Longe, left the expedition at Hardscrabble.

Dick Wootton, well-known mountain man in the Colorado Rockies, claimed that he joined the expedition at Hardscrabble but turned back when he saw the depth of the snow. Wootton had a buffalo farm west of El Pueblo during the 1840s. Some accounts relate that two men tried to join the expedition at Pueblo, but Frémont refused their services. Wootton may have been one of these.

Although Bill Williams and Ben Kern survived the ordeal in the mountains, they were murdered later while trying to retrieve some of the abandoned baggage. They returned to the San Luis Valley in late February 1849 with eight New Mexican settlers. According to the New Mexicans, Kern and Williams were killed on March 21 at the location of the cache by Utes retaliating for an attack on their band by the Whittlesey patrol. Edward Kern, guided by Antoine Leroux, retrieved his brother's body and some equipment. Uncertainty surrounds the disposition of Bill Williams's body. Although the Indians did have articles of clothing from the cache, some of the Kern brothers' personal belongings surfaced among the settlers of Abiquiu, Mora, and Rio Colorado. Just how or when the settlers acquired the equipment and personal effects was never determined, as those accused of possessing stolen property disappeared after being released into the custody of local officials.

Charles Taplin returned to the San Luis Valley with the Gunnison expedition in 1853. After nursing Gunnison back to health by feeding him *atole*, which also had been used to revive the men of Frémont's fourth expedition, Taplin, now claiming poor health, left the Gunnison expedition and headed for Taos. Perhaps the memory of the 1848-49 tragedy was too vivid. Taplin died two years later in Texas.

Richard Kern and Frederick Creutzfeldt, along with Captain John W. Gunnison and several members of his expedition, were killed near Sevier Lake in Utah, either by Indians or by men dressed as Indians (Hugh Gunnison, unpublished paper, Colorado State College, 1962). Lieutenant Beckwith completed Gunnison's work and filed the official report of the survey with J. H. Simpson. Lithographs for the Gunnison report were made from Richard Kern's sketches, which included scenes in the San Luis Valley.

The primary sources reproduced in Hafen and Hafen's *Frémont's Fourth Expedition*, Charles Preuss's diary, and the footnotes in Spence's volume 3 of *The Expeditions of John Charles Frémont* give additional information about the men who composed the roster of the fourth expedition.

2

The reconstruction of the route of Frémont's fourth expedition has depended upon the known primary sources. The Kern brothers' diaries, which are in the Huntington Library, San Marino, California, are available on microfilm. Colorado historian LeRoy R. Hafen compiled most of the diaries, letters, and memoirs associated with the expedition into *Frémont's Fourth Expedition*, volume 2 of the Far West and the Rockies series. The collection of Charles Preuss's diaries, *Exploring with Frémont*, edited by Erwin and Elisabeth Gudde, was published by the University of Oklahoma Press in 1958.

Micajah McGehee's account of the expedition is interesting reading, but it was written by a brother who based the story upon information in McGehee's journal (now in the library of Louisiana State University). Literary editing may have produced some of the discrepancies that appear in the *Century Magazine*.

Thomas Martin's and Thomas Breckenridge's reminiscences contain firsthand information given years after the event. Variations exist between Breckenridge's first account, which appeared as an article by Will C. Ferril entitled "The Sole Survivor" in the *Rocky Mountain News* (August 30, 1891) and the version printed in *Cosmopolitan* magazine.

Readers as interested in historical details as in the pleasure of walking in Frémont's footsteps should consult sources listed in the bibliography for more background information about the attitudes, events, and people associated with the railroad explorations of the nineteenth century. Solomon Carvalho and John Gunnison gave good descriptions of the San Luis Valley in the mid-1800s. These and other original sources are available on microfilm or through interlibrary loan.

3

Today the 37th parallel marks the Colorado-New Mexico line. Frémont could not have determined his route precisely when he wrote from Big Timbers that he intended "to ascend the Del Norte to its head," but he would have known that passes through the Sangre de Cristo and San Juan mountains lie near the 37th and 38th parallels. These passes would have conformed to the plan to cross into California through Walker Pass. Such a route would have confirmed the possibility of building a central railroad line to the Pacific, an idea that had been promoted in Congress by Senator Thomas Hart Benton.

The economic conflicts between North and South that preceded the Civil War are reflected in the railroad surveys. During his earlier expeditions Frémont had explored northern routes, later used by pioneers migrating to the Oregon country. Jefferson Davis and other southerners were pushing for a southern route. An expedition under the command of E. F. Beale followed this southern route to California about the same time that Frémont was stranded in the San Juans. Beale lost most of his pack train when extremely cold weather hit New Mexico. After losing the rest of his animals to the heat of the Arizona desert, Beale recommended that the army use camels in the desert Southwest.

4

Weather statistics for the San Luis Valley, dating from the 1850s when the first settlers emigrated to the area, are on file at the National Weather Station, Alamosa, Colorado. A study of the weather patterns reveals that Frémont and his men faced a truly unique winter in 1848-49. While cold is traditional within the area after a storm, the records show that the extreme cold associated with the San Luis Valley does not occur normally until January. In most years during a twenty-year-period of weather statistics (1950-71), above-freezing temperatures were recorded until the last week in December, giving December an average daily temperature of twenty degrees.

Because the high mountains surrounding the San Luis Valley tend to deflect storms, the typical winter weather pattern for the valley is a stationary high. Observations on file at the Alamosa station state: "When one of these highs controls the weather, the sky is clear, the day temperatures are moderately high and remarkably uniform, and the nights cold but seldom excessively cold, except when the ground is covered with snow, and where the air drainage is poor." See Charles F. Marvin, "Climatic Summary of the U.S.--Western Colorado" (Washington, D.C.: Government Printing Office, 1933).

The lowest temperatures on record for the San Luis Valley have occurred after heavy snowfalls. Heavy snow is not normal for the months of October through December. Only four times in forty years did the snowfall exceed twelve inches during the month of December, the month during which the fourth expedition encountered two feet of snow on the valley floor in 1848. In the San Luis Valley the average snowfall for December is 5.6 inches with only 2.0 inches being the average at the centrally located Garnett station.

In the mountains along the west side of the valley, where Frémont's men faced such bitter cold and deep snows, the snow average is greater but not commonly of the depth experienced in 1848. The annual average snowfall on the Cochetopa is 45.2 inches with 5.5 inches the average for November, 6.6 inches the average for December, and 9.0 inches the average for January. Suggestions that Frémont would have fared better had he taken a route over Cumbres Pass to the south are without merit. The weather records show that the average annual snowfall for Cumbres Pass in the Conejos Mountains is 263.9 inches with 25.7 inches being the average for November, 41.1 inches for December, and 50.1 inches for January. Occasionally, heavy snows do occur in the San Luis Valley during October. In those years below-freezing temperatures are recorded as early as November. The cold keeps the valley shrouded in snow, which in turn reflects the sun's warmth, thus maintaining cold temperatures throughout the winter months. Apparently Frémont arrived in the San Luis Valley during such a winter.

Many residents of the San Luis Valley have wondered why explorers like Frémont and Pike entered the valley in winter. By January 1807, Pike was desperate for relief, which could come only from the Spanish settlements in northern New Mexico, but that does not explain his reasons for following the Arkansas River into the mountains in late fall instead of seeking a less harsh environment for the winter. The death of Frémont's son delayed the fourth expedition, but Frémont believed that the passes would be open through December, by which time he intended to be in the lower regions of Utah. The geographic position of the San Luis Valley within the United States may have caused Frémont, Pike, and others not familiar with winters in the high mountain valleys of the West to assume that the climate would be similiar to the mountains of Virginia and other eastern areas lying along the 37th and 38th parallels.

In 1973 a young man from Illinois, who had visited the Frémont camps during the summer as a member of the Prairie Trek Expeditions of Thoreau, New Mexico, appeared at the author's door the day after Christmas with the announcement that he and his companions were going to make a quick trip up Mesa Mountain to see the camps in winter. The idea that the area might be inaccessible had not occurred to them. Plans changed quickly when the young explorers awoke the next morning to find their vehicle's water, oil, and gas line frozen.

5

**Big Timbers**    Chouteau's Island was named for trapper Auguste P. Chouteau, who with Julius De Mun opened the alternate route of the Santa Fe Trail in 1815-16. The Chouteau-De Mun party trapped the headwaters of the Arkansas River while waiting for permission from the Spanish governor of New Mexico to enter the Sangre de Cristo Mountains. On May 23, 1817, the entire party was arrested and taken to Santa Fe. Furs and livestock were confiscated, and the men's lives were threatened. After forty-eight days of imprisonment, Chouteau, De Munn, and their colleagues were released upon being sentenced to forfeit all property except one horse each and to leave Spanish territory (Hiram M. Chittenden, *The American Fur Trade of the Far West*, 545).

In 1969 the author located in the files of the Colorado Historical Society library an old, undated map bearing handwritten notations indicating the spot where Chouteau and De Mun had been captured and acknowledging that the owner of the map had found an alternate route to Santa Fe. The signature on the map was unclear, but research revealed that it was a segment of the 1814 William Clark map, which combined the information acquired through the explorations of the Louisiana Territory with the Spanish maps of the Southwest (*A Map of Part of the Continent of North America*, Colorado Historical Society).

6

**Mormontown and El Pueblo**

English journalist George Frederick Ruxton traveled from Vera Cruz, Mexico, to the Rocky Mountains of Colorado in 1847. His journal of this Rocky Mountain adventure, and a fictionalized version of his life among the mountain men, *Life in the Far West*, give insight into activities in the Rocky Mountains during the 1840s. Ruxton noted that the Mormons did not break ice to provide water for their horses. Instead, they depended upon the animals' getting enough liquid by eating snow. As he had prophesied in his journal, Ruxton soon encountered dead horses along the trail. The snow did not contain enough moisture to curtail dehydration when the animals were stressed.

Ruxton, who had hoped to join a Frémont expedition, died in St. Louis before the fourth expedition departed. Andrew Cathcart, a former captain in the hussars who had been with another expedition, returned to St. Louis because his friend Ruxton had died. Still in St. Louis when the fourth expedition was being organized, Cathcart, taking Ruxton's place, became a member of the ill-fated expedition and experienced more of an adventure than he had anticipated.

7

Janet Lecompte's *Pueblo, Hardscrabble, Greenhorn: the Upper Arkansas, 1832-1856* gives an excellent description of these early communities and the

mountaineers who settled them. Micajah McGehee noted that the mountain men, who had already
moved for the winter from Hardscrabble to the
settlements at Pueblo when Frémont arrived, returned with Frémont to help the expedition prepare for the ascent into the mountains. Richard
Kern, however, stated that several families were
still living at Hardscrabble when Frémont arrived.

**Huérfano
Valley**

8

The Williams Fork of the Huérfano River heads in
the Wet Mountains west of Greenhorn Peak, which
was named for Cuerno Verde, the Comanche chieftain defeated by Juan Bautista de Anza's forces in
1779. As the expedition moved along the creek,
the west slope of the stream's deep valley would
have blocked the view of Médano and Mosca passes,
which are so evident from both the Wet Mountain
and San Luis valleys. The detour over the mountains and through the snow-choked valleys expended
valuable time, energy, and food. The Huérfano
Valley could have been attained more easily by
moving southwest from El Pueblo along Charles
Autobees's Greenhorn Trail or by traveling either
from Bent's Fort or El Pueblo to the Huérfano Butte
and then following the Huérfano River into its
canyon.

9

Huérfano Butte, marking the trail to Mosca and
Sangre de Cristo passes, is the intersection of two
radiating volcanic dikes. The similar-appearing
Gardner Butte is a series of remnants of ring dikes
with sedimentary intrusions. The Spanish Peaks
are fully visible slightly downstream, but Sheep
Mountain and Little Sheep Mountain block the view
from this location. Richard Kern's diary entry is
important in helping to pinpoint the route used to
reach the Huérfano drainage.

Dome-shaped Sheep and Little Sheep mountains
are lacoliths of finely crystalized granite that contains no quartz. The Spanish Peaks, which once

marked the northern boundary between New Spain and Louisiana, are stocks formed of similar material and have various names, including Huajatolla and Cumbres Española. A Richard Kern watercolor, which is part of a private collection, beautifully portrays the real Spanish Peaks as seen on November 17, 1848, when the expedition was still on the plains. The protruding rock wall through which the Huérfano River has cut its gap is a microcyanite sill (Burroughs, interview, 1983).

10

Mosca Pass, known as Robidoux Pass in the mid-1800s because of Antoine Robidoux's wagon road, is an example of confusion that arises from Anglicization of Spanish words. Early Hispanic settlers of northern New Mexico and southern Colorado referred to the pass as *Moscoso*, the name of the explorer who led De Soto's men westward in a futile attempt to intercept the Coronado expedition after De Soto's death. Most historians agree that Moscoso and his men traveled no farther west than Texas; however, a few Colorado historians have tried to associate a rock carving of a Maltese cross found in the Sangre de Cristo Mountains with Moscoso. Why the early settlers referred to the pass as Moscoso in uncertain, but they may have known enough history of early Spanish explorations to want to honor that explorer.

In the 1870s the pass became known as Mosca Pass to the hundreds of gold- and land-hungry pioneers entering the San Luis Valley from the east. At least one historian has suggested that the name was associated with the Spanish word *mosca* because there were many flies or mosquitoes along the route. The mosquito population within the San Luis Valley was noted by explorers Gunnison, Heap, and Anderson, who wrote that while these insects were a nuisance near watercourses, the drier areas of the valley were virtually mosquito-free. More likely the name *Mosca* was either an Anglicization of Moscoso or a reference to an older meaning for *mosca*--"money in hand"--as a toll house had been built on the west side of the pass to collect fees from those who wished to use the road.

When interpreting Spanish words used for geographical features in the San Luis Valley and northern New Mexico, it is important to remember that isolation has preserved meanings and pronunciations that were common when settlers first came into the area. Modern meanings and new words created for a changing world often are unknown in rural areas where Spanish is passed from one generation to the next in conversational form.

11

Zebulon Pike's description is as accurate today as when he wrote in his diary: "The sand hills extended up and down at the foot of the White Mountains, about fifteen miles, and appeared to be about five miles in width. Their appearance was exactly that of the sea in a storm (except as to color), not the least sign of vegetation existing thereon."

Framed by Médano and Mosca passes, the 1,500-foot-high dunes have been created and sustained by southwest winds carrying the ancient silts and sands of the meandering Rio Grande, which has migrated from a course nearer the dunes to Alamosa, Colorado. As the winds sweep upward over the mountains and through the passes, the airborne debris is dropped to form the spectacular transverse dunes that comprise the Great Sand Dunes National Monument.

12

**Sand Hills**

The open character of Médano Pass surely has enticed foot travelers since the times of ancient peoples, as indicated by the Folsom sites near the sand hills. Zebulon Pike crossed Médano Pass from the Wet Mountain Valley into the San Luis Valley on January 28, 1807. Although it is not suitable for modern roads because sand chokes the west side, Frémont, after crossing the pass in 1853, decided that it would be practicable for a railroad route. A

4x4 road through the pass makes it possible to move from the Wet Mountain Valley into the San Luis Valley today. Travelers should move from east to west, as tires must be deflated to cross the sand. An air pump at the Great Sand Dunes National Monument allows tires to be reinflated.

Spanish-speaking settlers of the San Luis Valley pronounced the name of the pass with an accent on the next-to-last syllable with a tilde over the *n*, *medaño*. This older pronunciation is of Portuguese derivation, which is interesting since Oñate brought several Portuguese colonists with him to the San Gabriel settlement in northern New Mexico in 1598. In Germany the word is pronounced *medano* without the tilde (Eberhardt, interview, 1987). Modern Spanish pronunciation places the accent on the first syllable with no tilde. Either pronunciation refers to the sand hills found at the foot of the pass (Neamon, interview, 1986).

The entries in Charles Preuss's diary make clear the extent of the hardships upon men and mules in passing through the eastern range. Frederick Dellenbaugh was the first historian to note that Williams had failed to take the more direct route into the San Luis Valley. Dellenbaugh claimed that had the expedition crossed into the Wet Mountain Valley and followed Grape Creek to its source, the men would have reached Médano Pass within two days. While Médano Pass is obvious from both the San Luis Valley and the Wet Mountain Valley, it is not visible from the route over Promontory Divide into the Williams Creek Valley. This would explain why Frémont was not aware of the pass until he crossed into the San Luis Valley.

13

**Crestone Creek**

The name changes for the Rio de Tres Tetones that took place during the latter half of the nineteenth century are fascinating. As early as the seventeenth century, the Trois Tétons or Tres Tetones of the Sangre de Cristo Mountains marked the boundary between French and Spanish territories. The Spanish name continued to be used by many explorers and mountain men after the United States acquired first the French territory and later the Spanish-Mexican lands; however, some cartographers as late as the Gunnison expedition used the French version in referring to the stream, which had several tributaries heading among the three great peaks. As more maps of the western territories were made to enhance new expeditions, and as the interest in land development increased, the name of the stream became distorted. One can imagine an eastern cartographer struggling by dim light to decipher unfamiliar words.

First *Tres* was changed to *Cres*, which still was kept as a separate word. Another mapmaker must have been at least familiar with the meaning if not with the spelling of the creek's name and labeled the stream the Rio de Trois Teits. Apparently the next cartographer either was shocked by this anatomical reference or had a problem reading foreign words, as the next map identifies the flow as Christian Creek.

About this time miners started moving into the area, and the creek became known as Crestones. Eventually the final *s* was dropped. During this same period the peaks were undergoing name changes as well. Crofutt's map of 1885 indicates a Crestone Peak at 14,233 feet with Tres Tetones to the south at 14,198 feet. Oddly, in spite of all the changes, the current name is as appropriate for the area as was the first. The three great peaks, the *tétons*, still dominate the skyline, but numerous *crestones*, veins or outcroppings of minerals, continue to attract the interest of commercial explorers. In 1987 the Tres Tetones again endured another change with the addition of the name Challenger Point, in honor of the space shuttle crew.

The ample cottonwood stands and game along the several forks of the stream have made it a favorite stopping place for centuries as attested by the number of archaeological artifacts and sites found throughout the area. The numerous accounts by early travelers passing through the San Luis Valley refer to the lack of firewood on the valley floor; therefore, the timber was appreciated by historic travelers as well as their predecessors.

14

In moving west-northwest from their camp on the small stream north of the sand hills, the expedition paralleled the main course of the Rio Grande, which was over thirty miles to the south. The stream intersected and described as a "headwater of the del Norte" had to be the Saguache-San Luis flow. Normally travelers along the east side of the San Luis Valley would have moved farther north to Leroux Creek (Rito Alto) before cutting across the valley toward the entrance to Saguache Canyon, which appears clearly as a wide-open passage through the mountains. By cutting directly toward this opening, the fourth expedition failed to avoid the marshlands east of Moffat.

15

Since the San Juan Mountains had been hidden for two days by a cloud of ice crystals, it seems virtually impossible that Frémont could have seen the gap of the Rio Grande approximately thirty miles to the south and moved toward it. The one-mile-wide gap of the Rio Grande had been so obvious to Pike from the summit of Cerro de Ojito at the mouth of the Conejos that he referred to being able to see the Rio Grande gushing from the mountains; however, the peaks lying to the west, which form the Continental Divide near Wolf Creek Pass, are so prominent that they deny to the upper Rio Grande Valley the openness that is evident at the gap of the Saguache.

16

Gwinn Harris Heap, who was a member of E. F. Beale's 1853 expedition through the San Luis Valley, explained that the entire complex of passes on the upper Saguache was named Coochatope [Cochetopa] or "Gateway" because the entrance to each pass was marked by a distinctive rock formation. Nineteenth-century explorers, including Frémont, Gunnison, and Heap, used the spellings *Coochatope* or *Coochetopa*. Antoine Leroux, who regularly took wagonloads of trade goods through the area, wrote the word as *Cuchitohe*. In an 1853 report, Richard Kern also used a phonetical spelling, *Cuochutoha*.

The two main passes leading to the Western Slope tributaries of the Colorado or Grand River from the upper valley of the Saguache, meaning *blue earth* or *blue water*, were the Carnero and the "Cuimchipa," or Buffalo Pass, which is presently North Cochetopa Pass.

Heap's journal is the best source for identifying the original Carnero Pass. Nell's 1885 map of Colorado shows the road Heap would have used to travel from the Uncompahgre River through the Lake City country in his return to Fort Massachusetts. To save time, Heap reentered the San Luis Valley by way of Carnero Pass. He then followed the "Indian Trail" south to the Rio Grande and camped where the trail crossed the river about five miles east of the present site of Del Norte, Colorado. This ford, La Loma del Norte, had been used for centuries.

Heap asked his guides if they knew the route that Frémont had taken in 1848-49. Pointing to the sun setting behind Mesa Mountain, the men replied, "Puerto del Rio del Norte," which Heap interpreted as describing a late summer or fall pass reportedly discovered by Bill Williams; however, in a letter concerning the prospects of a central railroad route, Senator Thomas Hart Benton referred to a statement by Antoine Leroux that the Cochetopa was known among the Spanish-speaking New Mexicans as "El Puerto." Although Heap capitalized the phrase as though it were the name of a specific geographic feature, a linguist familiar with the colloquialisms of the area believes the phrase also could mean "he took the route north of the river" (Neamon, interview, 1981). Recent Rio Grande

Forest Service maps designate the road connecting the middle fork of Carnero Creek with the Mill Creek tributary of the Saguache as Carnero Pass. This road obviously does not fit the description given by Heap. The assignment of historically important names without careful research into exact locations creates numerous problems for historians and others interested in an area.

Further evidence that the Carnero was the southern pass of the Cochetopa complex is found in Gunnison's report. While Gunnison considered the northern route over the Cochetopa ideal to the extent that he recommended that no further exploration for a railroad route was necessary, he also noted, "It is possible, however, that the summit of the Carnero Pass, just south of the Coochatope [sic] may be more easily passed by a railroad than the latter; but this can only be determined by a minute survey." In spite of Gunnison's impression of the Cochetopa, consideration of the most open pass through the Colorado Rockies as a railroad route ceased for two reasons: Lieutenant Beckwith, who filed the official report, failed to submit an estimate of costs; and Gunnison's assessment of the pass was changed in J. H. Simpson's report to read simply that there should be no further exploration of this route. Secretary of War Jefferson Davis, who supported a southern route for a transcontinental railroad, agreed.

In the late 1800s four routes carried most of the traffic from the San Luis Valley to the west. Elwood Pass, at the head of Alamosa Creek, channeled prospectors and other travelers into the Durango area. The mine camps of Baker's Park were reached by following the Rio Grande to Spring Creek Pass or by crossing the Cochetopa passes. In 1874 Lieutenant George S. Anderson opened a route over Cumbres Pass in response to demands for access to gold fields in the Conejos Mountains. Only the Cumbres route accommodated a railroad, which is still in operation as the Cumbres and Toltec Scenic Railroad.

John Lawrence, who used the Cochetopa roads to haul poles, was one of the founders of Saguache, as was Otto Mears, who developed several roads, including those over Poncha Pass and the North Cochetopa, into Colorado's mining camps.

17
When the Saguache River floods, the excess water flows through the old channel of the river, which once cut south at the volcanic cliffs southeast of Saguache, Colorado, and then followed a course three miles east of U.S. Highway 285 along the western side of the San Luis Valley. Pike's crude drawing of January 1807 shows the Saguache in this course. The channel of the Saguache River has migrated to the northeast while the Rio Grande is moving toward the southwest (Burroughs, interview, 1983).

18
Although modern irrigation seizes the surface waters of Carnero and La Garita creeks, during flood stages subwaters of both tributaries follow old courses to form marshes and bogs where the rivers once would have merged with the Saguache.

According to George Ward, the Saguache once had a heavy growth of trees along its banks, but these were cut for buildings, fences, and firewood (Ward, interview, 1975). What may be the remnants of the timber along the Saguache can be found near the Mishak Lakes. Repeated checks by the author have shown that the distance at which a stand of trees is visible in the San Luis Valley is approximately seven miles. When Frémont's men reported trees along a river at seven miles distance, they were correct about the mileage, but the trees could not have been the forest along the main branch of the Rio Grande.

**Carnero Creek and Hell Gate**

19

LeRoy Hafen identified the old Indian trail along the west side of the San Luis Valley as Joaquin's Trail to associate it with the nickname of Antoine Leroux, who would have traveled this route carrying supplies to Robidoux's trading fort on the Uncompahgre River. The trail later was used by New Mexicans coming to settle the northern regions of the Guadalupe land grant. By the 1850s the trail was known as the Conejos Road. In 1861 Lafayette Head and John M. Francisco received a permit to operate the La Loma del Norte ferry where the trail had forded the Rio Grande for centuries.

John Lawrence would have used this road to carry goods from the Woodson store in Conejos to the new outpost of San Luis on the Saguache River. The establishment of a Woodson store on the Saguache undoubtedly encouraged travelers to abandon the Carnero Creek cutoff. Traces of the old Conejos road, which early Spanish-speaking travelers had marked with an etched stone, are still visible when new grass appears in the spring.

20

Biographers Bigelow and Upham, using Frémont's notes, state that the expedition was "North of the Del Norte Canon," which would fit with the location of Carnero Canyon and Hell Gate (Spence, *The Expeditions of John Charles Frémont*, 3:86). The canyon, marking the river's exit from the mountains, commences with three gaps, which have been cut through various volcanic materials. Farthest east are Fish Canyon ashflow tuffs from the La Garita caldera; next are several dikes radiating from the ancient Summer Coon volcano. The perpendicular walls of the largest gap, established in an east-tilting lava flow featuring vertical columnar jointing, are known as Hell Gate (Burroughs, interview, 1983). The narrow channel would have changed the flow of the water, keeping it from freezing solidly. The sheer cliff along the north side of the creek would force travelers to pass over the less formidable hills to the south. This route brought the expedition into Coolbroth Canyon, which resembles the main canyon of Carnero Creek. The head of Coolbroth Canyon lies in a more westerly direction while the Carnero flows from the west-north-west.

According to Frank White, Hell Gate was not named by the La Garita sheepherders, nor is there any Spanish name for this impressive formation. It has been known as Hell Gate since the first settlers appeared in the area (White, interview, 1980). Frémont's men might have deemed this name appropriate after their misfortunes.

21

**Cave Creek and Boot Mountain**

The small park feeding the headwaters of Poso Creek, another tributary of the south fork of the Carnero, leads to the upper valley of Cave Creek where numerous caves, carved in the Fish Canyon tuff by wind and water, line the canyon. Richard Kern entitled his watercolor "Proulx [sic] Creek" in honor of the first member of the expedition to perish. Proue died while the men were moving baggage toward the cache, which was near a stone wall of the same geologic formation located on La Garita Creek, the next stream to the south. Since the watercolors were completed and titled later, Richard may have confused the similarities of the two canyons, or he simply may have wished to honor the old explorer; however, snowy, twin-peaked Boot Mountain or Bole de Cuevas (Cave Creek's head), looms clearly in the background of the watercolor.

22

**Mesa Mountain**

The diary entries, noting the sudden descent into La Garita Creek's headwaters and the ascent into the park at the head of Perry Creek, are accurate, as is the entry "road over summits of hills," describing the east ridge of Mesa Mountain, which separates the tributaries of the Saguache and the tributaries of the La Garita. According to Frank White, the name *Rincon Quemado* or Burnt Creek was given to the creek in 1861 after the Utes set fire to the area in retaliation for an argument with the sheepherders (White, interview, 1980).

23

Had Frémont moved into Saguache Park as intended, he would have looked at the great dome of Mesa Mountain looming directly above him. Instead he found himself looking down onto the route he should have taken as the expedition struggled across the snowcapped summit.

Mesa Mountain and the cliffs at the heads of all the tributaries flowing from the mountain are Fish Canyon ashflow tuff, composed of biotite, hornblende, plagioclase, sanidine, and quartz latite with a 50-percent ratio of phenocrysts to the ground mass. This material issued from the La Garita caldera approximately 27.8 million years ago (Burroughs, interview, 1983).

Although higher than the Continental Divide, which is farther west, Mesa Mountain actually is the source of thirteen streams, all of which are tributary to the Rio Grande. Ridges running east and west lie above the bowl-shaped ampitheaters or cirques where the streams head and connect the broad summit of the mountain with other lower, less prominent dome-shaped summits named for the sheepmen who grazed their flocks in the late 1800s.

While Groundhog Creek heads amid gentle, grassy, spring-fed slopes, Deep Creek and Geban Creek have steep, talus-laden cliffs. The other streams have a pattern of cliffs on one side of the creek and a grassy slope on the other. Heavy growths of willows choke the banks of the streams as they flow toward the conifer forests.

The southwest winds build deep cornices of snow along the downwind side of the mountain while sweeping the grassy ridges almost snow-free.

24

Accounts of Williams's life and descriptions of the old mountaineer have been given by Edward Kern, Micajah McGehee, Alpheus Favour, and Frederic Voelker. Well known among the mountain men for his cunning, Williams could be an unscrupulous rascal, as seen in the articles George Ruxton wrote for British magazines. Prior to joining the fourth expedition, Williams had led the Reynolds expedition from Taos to Cumbres Pass, where they encountered Utes with whom Williams had lived until he took the Indians' pelts to Taos to sell and then squandered the money.

Williams had been with Frémont on the third expedition from August 28 until October 27, 1845, when he left because he did not want to cross the Sierra Nevada in winter. During the fourth expedition, Williams and Frémont argued over whether to follow the Carnero shortcut to the Cochetopa. An entry, which Favour states was in Williams's notebook--"I wanted to go one way and Frémont will go another and right here our troubles will commence"--almost sounds like a threat rather than a prophesy.

25

"Inscription Rock" was rediscovered by the author and Barbara Colville of Del Norte, Colorado, in 1975. During the 1930s, the Colorado Writers' Project had interviewed many early settlers of the San Luis Valley. Numerous pages of notes, still in original pencil copy, were in the files of the Colorado Historical Society in 1969. The author, while searching for information about the William Marshall expedition of 1874, read much of this material. Among the reminiscences were references to a rock at the head of Benino Creek upon which Frémont's men had left an inscription.

The first sheepherders came to the La Garita Mountains within ten years after Frémont's disaster. Some of them, like twenty-one-year-old Pedro

Valdez, father of La Garita herder Jesus Valdez, had been part of the rescue party that accompanied Alexis Godey (White, interview, 1980). These herders, who had found remnants of the upper Frémont camps as early as 1859, described a charred ledge between Perry and Geban creeks and told their children and grandchildren that Frémont's men had left writing on a rock at the head of Benino (or Reylas) Creek (White, *La Garita*, 1971).

Frank White's *La Garita*, which recounts his family's tales of finding evidence of Frémont's intrusion into the mountains at the heads of Geban, Benino, and Groundhog creeks, has provided a valuable reference source for San Luis Valley historians by citing the original Spanish names of creeks, domes, peaks, and valleys within the La Garita Mountains.

26

**Camp Dismal** Frank White stated that the mule bones dotting Mesa Mountain's slopes were forbidden as playthings because they were remnants of "animals that belonged to men who had died on the mountain." He recalled that the whitened bones of about half a dozen animals lay on the *banco* or terrace of Mesa Mountain above Rito del Cencho (Groundhog Creek), named for a boy killed there (White, interview, 1980). This location coincided with four skeletons discovered earlier during a Forest Service reconnaissance of the mountain in June 1980. Other skeletal remains have been found throughout the years in the Christmas Camp and at the heads of Embargo and Wannamaker creeks.

The first skeleton was found at the edge of the highest trees; the second, which had a broken skull, was near a young conifer; the third was located in the meadow just east of the head of Groundhog Creek; the fourth was on the ridge west of Groundhog Creek about three hundred yards from a small pond. The proximity and similar condition of the four skeletons made it unlikely that they were animals of herders or hunters and just happened to perish in the same area at about the same time.

The four skulls removed by Forest Service personnel were sent to Colorado State University for analysis. Weathering, loss of significant diagnostic characteristics, and the lack of museum collections or papers dealing with mules in the 1800s caused problems in definite identification. The first was identified as a female mule eight to twelve years old. The second was a male horse about five or six years old (though reference to Frémont's animals is usually to mules, some members of the expedition mentioned horses). The third was a female burro eight to ten years old. The fourth was a male horse eight to twelve years old.

Roger Anderson of the University of Denver examined the lichen colonies on the weathered bones. Eleven species of lichen were found to be present on one or more skulls. The rate of growth for lichen colonies varies according to species and climatic conditions; therefore, they can be used only to establish minimum age "because much weathering of the substrate may occur before a colony becomes established. Also, senile colonies can eventually flake off and be replaced by younger growths." The evidence from the lichen analysis did not prove that the four skulls retrieved from Mesa Mountain were the remains of Frémont's pack animals, but "it is compatible with this hypothesis" (Finley, correspondence, 1982).

27

George Ward, whose family homesteaded the upper Sagauche Valley after the Civil War, stated that the snow was always deeper between Dry Gulch and the south fork of the Wannamaker because it blew off the ridge and filled the cirque. Ward recalled four trees at the upper edge of the timber had been cut about twenty feet above the ground while shorter stumps were located deeper in the timber (Ward, interview, 1980).

28

As on most stumps in the Frémont camps, the ax marks are short and irregular, indicating that the trees were hacked rather than chopped. Charles Elliott's recollections of the height and location of the stumps were valuable in confirming the Wannamaker camp. Elliott also recalled two stumps fallen across each other to form a large X in the grass. Although the author and Elliott searched the area carefully in 1980, this distinctive feature could not be relocated. Later the author found a slide of those stumps that she had taken during a previous visit to the Wannamaker camp (Elliott, interview, 1980).

Pfeiffer discovered the Wannamaker camp while building a wagon road that followed Wannamaker Creek to the mine at Sky City and then continued over the ridge onto the Embargo Creek drainage. The traces of this road, still visible on the Wannamaker side, are used part way as a 4x4 road. Pfeiffer's road made it easy for someone to haul away the skeletal remains in George Ward's cairn.

According to Ward, Ray Woodard ran sheep at the head of Wannamaker Creek for a number of years. The Wannamaker drainage was turned into a cattle range after 1939 (Ward, interview, 1980).

29

**Christmas Camp**

Because Albert Pfeiffer, Jr., discovered the Christmas Camp first, he called it Camp 1. When he later came across the Wannamaker camp, he referred to it as Camp 2. This numbering has caused confusion at least among local residents, who have assumed that the chronology refers to the order of occupation by Frémont's men. When historians following Allan Nevins's lead tried to route the expedition up any of the south- or west-flowing tributaries of the Rio Grande, they found reinforcement for their routes in Pfeiffer's numbering.

30

In 1930 forest ranger E. S. Ericson and Epimenio
Romero, a sheepherder, found the handmade sledge
runners. One sledge was four feet long, the other
six or seven feet. By 1930 only a runner and the
cross pieces of the larger sledge remained. Ericson
searched the area and found two pieces of leather
and a piece of hardwood among the stumps standing six to eight feet high. Ericson marked the site
as the Christmas Camp. Ruth Marie Colville, the
Charles Bococks, Al Hibbs, and Elizabeth and
Richard Conour later helped Ratliff retrieve the
remnants of the sledges.

Many people find it difficult to believe that evidence of the Frémont expedition has lasted all these
years. While wood and bone deteriorate within a
few decades in a warmer environment, the cold
climate and rarified air above 12,000 feet tend to
preserve artifacts rather than destroy them.
However, within the past few years, stumps that
had stood for over 135 years seem to have exploded
from within. Silvery fragments of pulverized wood
lie where once had been a weathered but intact
stump.

Hunters, hikers, and campers have contributed
to greater destruction of the Frémont camps than
have time and weather. In 1977 the author and
members of the Prairie Trek Expeditions discovered extensive desecration of the Christmas Camp
by a hunting party that had used several of the
stumps for firewood. The charcoal and rock debris of seven large campfires filled the site, and
empty beer cans littered the ground where Frémont's
men had hoped for relief from their ordeal.

31

George Ward also commented that he had been
told since childhood that the expedition had moved
down Groundhog and La Garita creeks after trying
Myers (Embargo) Creek (Ward, interview, 1980).

## 32

**Groundhog Creek Camps**

While stumps can be found at the heads of several creeks heading on Mesa Mountain, either the terrain does not fit the description in the Kerns' diaries or the stumps do not have the same characteristics as those found in the Christmas Camp.

The stands at the heads of South Carnero Creek and Geban Creek were examined in 1973 and again in 1974. The South Carnero stumps appear to be an old timber cut. The steep-sided, talus-covered cliffs at the head of Geban Creek do not match the parklike approach to Mesa Mountain described in the diaries. During the late 1800s considerable prospecting occurred near the headwaters of Geban Creek where erosion had exposed intrusions and veins in the volcanic materials. A legend that either sacks of gold or gold bars were found along the creek's upper slopes reinforced the treasure tales connected with the LeBlanc family. Early residents of the La Garita-Del Norte area named the creek Geban because a French military jacket (*gabán*) had been found at its head.

## 33

**Point of Rocks**

Among the Kern effects David Weber found a letter from Edward Kern to an unknown person bearing the date April 30, 1858. The letter refers to sketches made during the fourth expedition and reads in part: "The other sketch 'the point of Rock,' Proulx' [*sic*] Creek was made by my diary Jany 11 1849." It continues: "I called the place at the time, the Creek after Proulx, the first of our party who perished, and the Point of Rocks, was so known among the men, it being a remarkable land mark for any who might return in search of the effects of the expedition, as there was a large cache near that place--Subsequently (in endeavoring to recover the property of the Expedition) at this place were killed Dr. Benjamin J. Kern and our guide William S. Williams."

The fourth expedition was the best outfitted expedition to enter the West, as St. Louis business-men had provided Frémont with the latest and best in camp equipment. Among the gear mentioned by the Kern brothers, McGehee, and Thomas Martin, which might have been left at the cache, were sketchpads, presses for preserving specimens, a revolver, powder flask, ramrod, soap, barometer, keg of powder, skillet, medicines, trade items, summer coat, thermometer, leggings, two kitchens, mittens, moccasins, hat, boots, bedding, overcoat, pot lids, knives, kettles, spades, rifles, a gilt-edged Bible, and tin dinner plates.

When the expedition left St. Louis, included in the baggage were two cases of amputory instru-ments, chronometers, a sextant, a refractory tele-scope, compasses, a two-foot telescope on a tran-sit, picket stakes, tool boxes, barrels, trunks, bits and stirrups, muleshoe iron, and blacksmith tools (according to Mary Lee Spence, Stepperfeldt was a blacksmith).

Riding saddles were lost on the mountain, as were the cross-tree packsaddles furnished by Thornton Grimsley Company of St. Louis, the de-signer of the dragoon saddle that had been made to order for the military. The camp gear had been furnished by O. D. Filley, copper and tinsmith of St. Louis, probably in hopes of a government contract if the expedition were successful (*Western Jour-nal* . . . , 1848; St. Louis city directory, 1848). Mar-tin referred to rubber covers fourteen feet by six-teen feet, which undoubtedly were used to wrap the seventy-pound bundles transported from the mountain to the cache.

Tents and ropes, pads, blankets, parfleches, snowshoe strings, rawhide lariats, and candles either were eaten by the mules or consumed by the men during their exodus.

34

**The Rescue Parties**

Tom Breckenridge's tale first appeared in the *Rocky Mountain News* of August 30, 1891. Entitled "The Sole Survivor," this account varies slightly from the *Cosmopolitan* article, which added fanciful details such as the Christmas Day menu.

Breckenridge and his family appeared in Telluride in 1878, when the area began humming with mining activities. At first their names were listed in county records as "Brackenridge," the same spelling used by Frémont in a letter to his wife, Jessie. Breckenridge had several claims, including the Hattie, Keno, and Royal lodes. He relinquished all these properties to the State of Colorado in 1881.

The Breckenridges reappeared in the Telluride area in the 1890s. This time, the sons were operating as packers and freighters. Ore from the mines was transported to the railhead at Alamosa in the San Luis Valley. According to San Miguel County tax records, Tom Breckenridge's home in 1891, when he reminisced about the fourth expedition, was located in the small mining camp of San Miguel about three miles downstream from Telluride. His tax of $11.42 was not paid, and Breckenridge's name disappeared from the county records after that date.

The ups and downs of mining camps continued to affect Breckenridge's family as Walter C., Dee, and Reece B. Breckenridge, listed as residents of West Telluride, bought and sold mules and wagons throughout the 1890s. Records seem to indicate that Mrs. C. E. Breckenridge was a widow who experienced hard times as she repeatedly sold and redeemed her household furniture. An Irene Breckenridge was enrolled in the Telluride school in 1895, but the Breckenridge family later disappeared from the area.

A letter to R. W. Settle from Joe Hyatt Hume, a nephew of Breckenridge, also confirms the story of Breckenridge's having killed the deer.

35
The road along the north side of the Rio Grande above Del Norte was laid in 1874 by the residents of the settlement of Loma. This small community, where William Henry Jackson stayed during his photographic expedition to the San Juan Moun-

tains, competed with Del Norte for the post office and other official recognition. Each town started building a road westward along the river with the hope of prospering from the heavy traffic to the Creede mining district. The settlers had agreed that whichever rival reached Creede first would become the sole community. The residents of Loma ran out of money as their road approached the confluence of the Rio Grande and its south fork. The town was abandoned, and the residents moved across the river to become citizens of Del Norte (Del Norte file, Kings Daughters Library, 1968).

36
Tony Valdez, an early settler of the Del Norte area, recalled that the Indian who assisted Frémont was known locally as Chief San Juan (Del Norte file, Kings Daughters Library, 1968). Although Preuss used only the singular--Indian--to describe this encounter, another variation states that Frémont's party met a band of fourteen or fifteen hunters, which seems possible, and one Indian was assigned to guide the men to the New Mexican settlements. Frémont, who gave his blankets and possibly his rifle to the Indian in exchange for assistance, reported that the Indian was the son of a Grand River chieftain whom he had met on a previous expedition. There can be little doubt that the rescue of the original relief party and possibly the salvation of the men left behind were due to the assistance Frémont received from the unidentified Indian.

37
Several villages had been established along the Rio Colorado or Red River and other tributaries of the Rio Grande north of Taos. El Rito, Questa, San Cristobal, Arroyo Hondo, and Taos are among the settlements that trace their histories to the early days of the Trappers' Trail, which led through the southern San Luis Valley.

**The Relief
Camps**

38

The first settlement on the Conejos was San Francisco, established in 1832 at the confluence of the San Antonio and Conejos rivers by the one hundred families who received the Guadalupe Land Grant. These first families were driven from their homes by Kiowa Indians, who claimed the area for hunting and gathering willows. A second settlement in 1842, San Margarita (correct Spanish is Santa Margarita), met a similar fate. In an attempt to meet the requirements of the grant, the original settlers or their descendants began as early as 1846 to establish summer settlements like Servietta. During the summer months the grantees would graze stock throughout the San Luis Valley while tending fields of corn and peas. After the fall roundup, the crops would be harvested and enough seed cached for the next spring's planting. The settlers then returned to New Mexico, thus avoiding harsh winters and confrontation with the Indians (Richmond, "La Loma de San Jose," 1969).

In 1848, after reaching an agreement with the Ute Indians, Tata Atanasio Trujillo brought settlers from the Red River settlements to the Conejos River and established the village of Rincones (*San Luis Valley Historian*, 8, No. 4, 1976). Frémont's contacts with Taos residents may have made him aware of the attempts to settle the San Luis Valley; thus, his instructions to his men to head for "Rabbit River"--the Conejos. Thomas Martin recalled that they were to head for a settlement on the Conejos named Socorro. No record exists for such a settlement, but Martin may have confused the Spanish word for "relief" with another settlement's name.

39

The Spaniards were correct in naming Sierra Blanca, as it is not a singular mountain but a short range with six peaks, four of which exceed 14,000 feet. Sierra Blanca, composed of materials of volcanic origin, drifted from the southwest and collided with the Sangre de Cristo Mountains (Burroughs, interview, 1983).

The mountain in Richard Kern's watercolor *The Relief Camp*, part of the Amon Carter collection, does not look exactly like the Sierra Blanca but instead resembles Tres Tetones farther north. This inconsistency created a problem in confirming the location of the relief camp because Kern's representations of geographic features had been so accurate in other works. Taos artist Helen Blumenschein resolved the discrepancy when she noticed a fine pencil line to the right of the high peak that dominates the watercolor. Kern had sketched the mountain accurately but had made the highest peak of the sierra, Blanca Peak, more prominent and formidable by failing to paint in some of the lower peaks.

**The Reunion**

40
The distances between the early settlements of the San Luis Valley and northern New Mexico reflect an average day's travel by horse or wagon, which was fifteen to twenty miles.

41
William LeBlanc, who had purchased the "Taos Lightning" gin mill after the murder of Simeon Turley, had come to the area to search for buried treasure, as he reportedly had a map showing where the gold had been cached. The stories of the Frenchmen's treasure and the La Ventana treasure are similar in that both featured a Frenchman who survived an Indian attack and returned to France with a map showing the location of the hidden gold. LeBlanc was supposed to be a descendant of a Frenchman who had made such a map after his companions had been killed by Indians.

Antonio LeBlanc and José de La Luz LeBlanc were among the first settlers in the San Luis Valley. Antonio was a trader for the community of La Loma de San Jose, and José de La Luz founded the town of El Doctore northwest of Del Norte, Colorado (Richmond, "La Loma de San Jose"). With their relatives and friends, they organized a company of stockholders to continue the search for the hidden gold. William LeBlanc was undoubtedly the "Le Blond" whom John Greiner stated helped retrieve Ben Kern's body from the San Juan Mountains.

42

One question asked frequently is: Why did Frémont take new recruits with him while leaving behind men who had proven their ability to endure the hardships of western exploration? Stepperfeldt, whose health had been affected severely, chose to return to his home in Illinois and carried the first descriptive account of the disaster to reach the eastern newspapers. Cathcart, who described himself as "a perfect skeleton" in a letter to a friend, expressed a desire to return to Scotland after a period of recuperation (Spence, *The Expeditions of John Charles Frémont*, 3:66).

Frémont's break with Williams had to be based in part on Frémont's belief that the guide was responsible for the disaster that had befallen the expedition. In a letter to his wife, Jessie, Frémont condemned Williams for either having forgotten the route or never having known the trail in the first place. Some historians have argued that Frémont failed to follow Williams's advice, but Preuss's diary states that he and Frémont were behind the expedition when Williams turned away from the Cochetopa and headed toward the south. After the conference on the plain, which was mentioned by several members of the expedition, Godey and Preuss urged Frémont to follow Williams toward the promised snow-free tableland. In a letter written to Antoine Robidoux, Edward Kern confirmed that Williams had led the expedition into the mountains by what was supposed to have been Robidoux's road to his trading fort on the Uncompahgre.

Werner Eberhardt of Cincinnati, Ohio, currently

is retranslating Charles Preuss's diaries. By enlarging copies of the original manuscript, Eberhardt has been able to interpret sentences and phrases that were heretofore unclear. He states that one such sentence, "Er verlor hier schon viel von seinen Boden," which the Guddes omit, translates literally as "Here already he [Williams] lost much of his ground." In Germany, this expression would be used during an event like an earthquake or to describe someone who had become disoriented.

Williams's reputation lay in knowing the mountains of southern Colorado. For most of his sixty-one years he had roamed the wilderness and had survived through a craftiness that was legendary. Historians who have assigned to Williams the responsibility for choosing the disastrous route have suggested that by the winter of 1848 the old mountaineer had become senile or that the deep snow had caused him to become confused. For years this author accepted the latter explanation. The departure from the river, the snow, belly-deep on the mules, or both, might have disoriented Williams, causing him to pursue a course along Coolbroth Canyon rather than following the south fork of the Carnero to Moon Pass and then descending into the upper Saguache Valley. Possibly the aging guide had not realized his error until the expedition was struggling toward the snowy summit of the mountain instead of moving through the expected open pass.

In the fall of 1980, during an excursion to the Wannamaker camp, the author started walking through the buckbrush along the ridge leading from the headwaters of Wannamaker Creek toward Palmer Mesa, just as Charles Preuss's small party would have done. Suddenly it became obvious to her that this was an excellent summer route, or as Heap noted, a good fall pass, from the San Luis Valley to the headwaters of the Cochetopa Creek.

A conversation with George Ward that evening revealed that he believed that Williams was leading the expedition across the high country toward

Spring Creek Pass at the head of the Rio Grande. While a trail across the virtually level ridges of Mesa Mountain and Palmer Mesa would be a good late summer route, avoiding bogs, marshes, and mosquitoes along swollen creeks, no knowledgeable mountaineer would go over a mountain in winter instead of through a good, open pass--especially with a pack train. That, however, was exactly what Williams had done.

Having traveled the route through the mountains on both sides of the San Luis Valley, the author realized that although every trail chosen by Williams led toward Frémont's objectives, not a single one was the best choice. Williams consistently ignored better routes in favor of steep, snow-choked canyons and detours, causing hardships and delays that eventually resulted in exhaustion, hypothermia, and death for men and animals.

Had Williams deliberately sabotaged the expedition? The trail over Mesa Mountain would not have been traveled as regularly as the roads through the Cochetopa complex. Since the chance of anyone accidentally coming across abandoned baggage would have been slim, come spring Williams would have been able to retrieve $8,000 to $10,000 worth of gear (Hafen and Hafen, *Frémont's Fourth Expedition*, 221). Also, the period prior to the Civil War was filled with intrigues by government officials and private citizens who pushed for the economic development of their states or regions. Some southerners, promoting a southern railroad line, would have been gratified had Frémont's quest for a central route to the Pacific failed. Williams's motives for choosing the route followed by the fourth expedition might never be known, but this author believes the evidence of the route itself may suggest that he hoped to profit from the failure of the expedition.

The allegation of cannibalism also had to have influenced Frémont's decision to break with Williams. Preuss noted in his diary that the surviving members of the rescue party had fed upon King's

body. In a letter to R. W. Settle, one of Breckenridge's relatives confirmed Preuss's entry--"The tale
in my family is they had been forced to eat the
dead before the deer was killed by Uncle Tom"
(Hume, letter, 1937). Both Senator Benton and his
daughter Jessie accused Williams of cannibalism,
and Jessie claimed that Kit Carson had stated that
no man turned his back on Williams in hard times.
Although Frémont never mentioned the subject in
any correspondence, Carvalho wrote that Frémont
called together the men of the fifth expedition when
they were caught by a blizzard. After describing
the ordeals of the previous expedition, Frémont
threatened to shoot the first man who "made or
hinted at such a proposition" (Carvalho, *Incidents
of Travel and Adventure*, 164).

The other three members left in Taos, the Kern
brothers, certainly did not anticipate Frémont's action. In a letter to his sister Mary, Edward Kern
revealed a feeling of betrayal: "He [Frémont] has
broken faith with all of us" (Hafen and Hafen,
*Frémont's Fourth Expedition*, 224). Edward's letters
do provide some insights into reasons for the break,
which must have been especially humiliating for
him since he played an important role during the
third expedition's conquest of California.

Clearly antagonisms had developed between the
Kerns and other members of the expedition during
the months in the mountains. Solomon Carvalho's
account of the fifth expedition reveals a prejudice
by educated "gentlemen of science" toward the
rugged ruffians of the frontier, who composed the
working force of any expedition. Edward Kern's
remark to Mary that he and his brothers had been
reduced to being muleteers, which was "cutting to
our dignity," exhibited this same social snobbery.
Kern further criticized Frémont for choosing to
associate with those who should have been his in-
feriors while failing to extend to the Kerns the respect
that was their due. Apparently the Kerns had considered themselves above menial tasks. Anticipat-
ing the return of the rescue party with fresh pack

animals, the brothers had waited in the Groundhog Creek camp while the rest of the men, following
Frémont's orders, had dragged the heavy bundles
to the cache before starting toward the settlements.
Edward Kern wrote later, "Not that any of us were
unwilling to assist in any work *if necessity* required
it--but this was not the case" (ibid., 227).

Edward Kern also mentioned that a "very natural" dislike had developed between his brother Ben
and Frémont. Possibly Frémont considered Ben's
petulance, as revealed through his constant references to despair and gloom, to be demoralizing
and detrimental to the success of the expedition.
No doubt Frémont, who seemed to get along well
with many of the individualists who penetrated
the western wilderness, would have felt frustrated
in dealing with Ben's temperamental behavior.
Edward claimed that the problem stemmed from
Frémont's being jealous of anyone having knowledge equal to his own.

A possible reason for the break in Frémont's
relationship with the Kerns may be found in Edward's statement that Frémont had preferred to
believe "lies carried to him by others prejudicial to
us" (ibid.). Although Edward had tried to place
responsibility for Raphael Proue's death on harsh
treatment by Frémont, the other men undoubtedly
attributed their comrades' deaths to what they
perceived as the Kerns' dawdling and stated such
opinions when they were reunited with Frémont.
Definitely Lorenzo Vinsonhaler and Thomas Martin were among those feeling animosity toward the
Kerns. Martin admitted that twice he advised
Vinsonhaler to strike for the settlements and leave
the Kerns behind. The enmity between the Kerns
and Vinsonhaler was noted in Richard Kern's diary
and later in Edward Kern's letters.

Any stories carried by Vinsonhaler would have
justified his actions at the expense of the Kerns.
One of the stories had to be that the Kerns had
resorted to cannibalism. Visonhaler reported to
Frémont that the expedition had disbanded "in order

to prevent them [the men] from living upon each other." This was the rationale for having the men move downriver as rapidly as possible, leaving faltering comrades with the last comfort of a fire. Apparently Vinsonhaler had some justification for his belief. The Indians of the expedition, frightened by threats to kill and eat them, had left the Kerns' mess and joined Vinsonhaler's group. Charles Taplin told Vinsonhaler that the weaker members intended "to remain where they were until the relief should come, and in the meantime to live upon those who had died, and upon the weaker ones as they should die." Taplin may have decided to stay with the weaker members as a hunter in hopes of deterring their plan. Andrew Cathcart, a member of the weaker party, also disclosed that "some of the survivors fed on dead bodies of comrades. I saw some awful scenes" (Spence, *The Expeditions of John Charles Frémont*, 3:91).

One of the greatest discrepancies in the information about the expedition lies in accounts concerning the deaths of Andrews and Rohrer. On January 23, his last entry before being rescued, Richard Kern wrote in his original diary, "Andrews & Rohrer supposed to be dead." This would seem to indicate that Richard had not seen their corpses. In Richard's revised diary, which Stepperfeldt carried to the *Quincy* (Ill.) *Whig*, the entry reads, "January 22, Rohrer and Andrews did not come up." Vinsonhaler claimed that the Kerns had told him later that Andrews and Rohrer had wandered from camp and were not seen again. These statements contradict Micajah McGehee's account, which discloses that McGehee, Stepperfeldt, and Taplin were sitting by the fire when an unnamed member of the party, which had to be one of the Kerns or Cathcart, approached with the suggestion that the bodies of Andrews, who had died, and Rohrer, who was dying, be used to sustain life until relief arrived. McGehee urged the perpetrator of this proposition to wait three days before resorting to such an act. Since Godey arrived that third day, an assumption has been that members of the weaker party abided by McGehee's request and refrained from feeding upon the bodies of Andrews and Rohrer.

A comment in Edward Kern's second letter to his sister Mary, which was written during the time Ben Kern and Bill Williams were in the mountains attempting to retrieve the baggage after Frémont's departure from Taos, may sustain the charge leveled by Vinsonhaler and the others. The Kerns' first host in Taos had been Carlos Beaubien, owner of the Sangre de Cristo Land Grant, and Edward had lamented earlier about being fed only "soup and weak coffee." In the second letter, Edward described New Mexican village life and added, "Our food is good and for this country quite a satisfactory change from what it was a month ago, when hide ropes gun covers Wolf 'and mair thats horrible and awfu--'What e'en to name wad be unlawfu" (Hafen and Hafen, *Frémont's Fourth Expedition*, 228). During the exodus from the mountains, the Kerns and their comrades had eaten anything made of hide or leather, the decaying carcass of a wolf including the hair, even pinfeathers; and according to Richard Kern, they had searched for snails and worms. All of these might be considered *horrible and awful*; but only one source of food would have been *unlawful*--human flesh.

Cannibalism, though abhorrent, was accepted on the frontier for saving lives under drastic conditions. That the Kerns may have been guilty seems insufficient to have caused the break and the years of discord between them and Frémont since some others accused of feeding on the dead had continued to California. Undoubtedly much of the bitterness in Edward and Richard Kerns' letters reflected not only the frustration of being left in Taos but also anger over their brother Ben's murder. While the Kerns openly criticized Frémont, their friend Cathcart sent the Pathmarker a commemorative sword honoring his leadership capabilities. Even Preuss and Carvalho, both of whom complained about some of Frémont's eccentricities, praised his ability to hold the loyalty of his men under the worst of conditions. Frémont never alluded to his reasons for leaving the Kern brothers in Taos, and eventually both Richard and Edward resolved their differences with him.

43

The earliest recorded ford of the upper Rio Grande was by Don Diego de Vargas in 1694. After taking corn from the Pueblo Indians to feed hungry colonists in Santa Fe, Vargas and his men, fearful of being ambushed, had to find a different route back to their capital. The Rio Grande Gorge, which commences just below the Colorado-New Mexico line, forced the expedition to travel north into the San Luis Valley before crossing the Rio Grande near the present State Line Bridge.

The Conejos River has had at least three flood plains through the San Luis Hills. Indications appear that the river is continuing to migrate to the north as the elevations of the area around the San Luis Hills are altered by geologic action. Colorado Highway 142 from Manassa to the Rio Grande follows along one of the abandoned flood plains (Burroughs, interview, 1983).

44

The original settlement of San Acacio predates San Luis, which is officially recognized as Colorado's oldest community. The area now occupied by San Luis was known as *los jacales*--the sheds--suggesting that it may have been the location of the sheep camp which Carlos Beaubien ran on the Culebra after he inherited the Sangre de Cristo Land Grant. During the Ute uprising in 1855, settlers along the Culebra River fled from their homes and hid among the willows until danger passed. The residents of San Acacio then abandoned their homes, moved upstream where there was greater protection, and helped establish present San Luis.

45

The word *costilla* refers to the riblike formations of alluvium eroded from the Sangre de Cristo Mountains. This geologic area, known as the Costilla Plain, is the eastern border of the treeless, basaltic expanses of the Taos Plateau, an area virtually without water except for the Rio Grande, which flows through a gorge hundreds of feet deep. The hills north of the alluvial deposits are called the Culebra Reentrant, the only true foothills in the San Luis Valley (Burroughs, interview, 1983).

46

The six hamlets were Taos, San Fernando, the Pueblo, La Placita, El Rancho, and El Ranchito. In 1853 a dragoon camp was located southwest of the hamlets. Several roads led from Taos, but all intersected with the Camino Real, connecting the northern frontier with Santa Fe, the oldest capital city in the United States. The present road south of Taos, which passes through the Rio Grande Gorge, was built between 1860 and 1875 by John Dunn (Blumenschien, interview, 1986).

The historic museums in Taos include the Blumenschein House (originally the home of Taos trapper Antoine Ledoux), William and Charles Bents' homes, the hacienda of Padre Antonio José Martinez, and Kit Carson's home.

Other "Sights and Sounds" to be enjoyed in the Taos area are the Fechin House, Millicent Rogers Museum, the Taos Art Center, which features plays and concerts, Fort Burgwin's summer lecture series, the library at the Harwood Foundation, petroglyphs and ruins along Pot Creek, the original "Camino Real" to Santa Fe, the Taos Valley ski area, and tours of art galleries and specialty shops.

While Taos is noted for its lodging and eating establishments, bed and breakfast and interesting workshops also are available through Las Palomas, once the home of Mable Dodge Luhan, the patron of D. H. Lawrence and other notable writers and artists who came to the area.

Although the author has relied almost exclusively on primary documents, such as the Kern diaries, for direct quotations in the text, much of the quoted material can be found in a few standard works available to the researcher. Chief among these are LeRoy R. and Ann W. Hafen, eds., *Frémont's Fourth Expedition* (hereinafter HAFEN & HAFEN) and Charles Preuss, *Exploring with Frémont*, translated and edited by Erwin G. and Elisabeth Gudde (hereinafter PREUSS). Where differences occur, the author has relied on her reading of the primary material. Complete citations, with the exception of those from the Foreword, are given in the Bibliography. The numbers at left refer to pages in this book on which citations appear.

vi "proved to be Frémont's 'Yale College and his Harvard'" William H. Goetzmann, *Army Exploration in the American West, 1803-1863*, 70.

viii "They say that as *Robinson Crusoe* is the most natural and interesting fiction of travel, so Frémont's report is the most romantically truthful." Jessie Benton Frémont to John C. Frémont, June 16, 1846 (NCC--Nevins Collection).

viii "an opportunity to improve myself [in] landscape painting" David J. Weber, *Richard H. Kern: Expeditionary Artist in the Far Southwest, 1848-1853*, 26.

xi "a pale intellectual looking young man . . . and dangers of the wilderness" Alfred S. Waugh, *Travels in Search of the Elephant* . . . Ed. John F. McDermott (St. Louis: Missouri Historical Society, 1951), 15.

xi "seen in no other man the qualities of lightness . . . in so perfect an equilibrium" Bayard Taylor, *Eldorado* (reprint, Palo Alto, 1968), 69-70.

xi "he had an eye like a falcon . . . but tinkling with merriment on slight provocation" John Raymond Howard, *Remembrance of Things Past* (New York, 1925), 82.

2    "children of Nature"   HAFEN & HAFEN, 294.

2    "a chilling prospect"   Micajah McGehee, typescript diary, 1848-49, LSU (hereinafter McGEHEE).

3    "spires of blue and scarlet to the very zenith"   McGEHEE.

6    "Friends, I don't want my bones to bleach upon those mountains this winter amidst that snow"   McGEHEE, although this appears in a slightly different form in HAFEN & HAFEN, 146.

8    "One broad, white, dreary-looking plain lay before us bounded by white mountains"   McGEHEE, although this appears in a slightly different form in HAFEN & HAFEN, 149.

9    "the line of the present expedition with one explored in 1848-49" John C. Frémont, "Letter to the Editors of the *National Intelligencer* . . ."

10   "an immense natural deer-park"   Solomon Carvalho, *Incidents of Travel and Adventure in the Far West* . . . (1954 edition), 141 (CARVALHO).

10   "travelled up the San Louis Valley, crossing the Rio Grande del Norte, and entered the Sarawatch Valley"   CARVALHO, 142.

10   "prairie-grass fields"   Lieut. E. G. Beckwith, "Report of Exploration for a Route for the Pacific Railroad . . . ," *Pacific Railroad Reports*, vol. 11, p. 44.

10   "low place of long grass weeds & cattails"   HAFEN & HAFEN, 98.

13   "rapid, rough-bottomed, but boggy streams"   HAFEN & HAFEN, 151.

14   "took up the Wahsatch"   HAFEN & HAFEN, 100.

15   "immense bald hill supposed to be the dividing ridge"   HAFEN & HAFEN, 125

16   "a snow-free tableland"   PREUSS, 144.

18   "wanted to die"   PREUSS, 145.

19    "frequent ineffectual attempts"   HAFEN & HAFEN, 153.

19    "lofty and dreary solitude"   HAFEN & HAFEN, 154.

19    "tried the stoutest hearts"   HAFEN & HAFEN, 102.

19    "deliverance or destruction"   HAFEN & HAFEN, 103.

20    "small fir grove"   PREUSS, 145.

20    all "ahead . . . was white, we decided to return"   PREUSS, 145.
      Eberhardt gives a slightly different variation.

20    "They returned   they returned"   HAFEN & HAFEN, 103.

20    "horror   desolation   despair"   HAFEN & HAFEN, 103.

24    "comfortable day"   HAFEN & HAFEN, 127.

25    too "troublesome" to bother   PREUSS, 147.

25    "The Colonel determined . . . to return by a different direction to
      the Rio Grande"   HAFEN & HAFEN, 155.

26    "we will have to retrace our steps back up a hard road & take
      another trail"   HAFEN & HAFEN, 105.

28    "novel loneliness"   HAFEN & HAFEN, 107.

28    "fired out the old year and passed the pleasantest night"   HAFEN
      & HAFEN, 128.

29    "We would move camp three or four miles at a time"   HAFEN &
      HAFEN, 156.

30    "good shanty finished for the storm"   HAFEN & HAFEN, 108.

30    "weak & dispirited"   HAFEN & HAFEN, 107.

30    cast a "hungry eye" at mice   HAFEN & HAFEN, 107.

30    "men passed on with loads"   HAFEN & HAFEN, 108.

32    "Moved towards the Col's camp [and] left early . . . to meet and hurry the mules"  HAFEN & HAFEN, 129.

32    "under the shelving rock below a cave"  HAFEN & HAFEN, 129.

32    "Between the last camps . . . against the severity of the storm"  HAFEN & HAFEN, 157.

32    "By this time, two others, Capt. Cathcart and R. Kern, arrived to take shelter from the storm. They had not a thing to eat, and we had our last portion."  HAFEN & HAFEN, 158.

32    "a cupful of boiled macaroni and a cup of sugar"  HAFEN & HAFEN, 158.

33    "the last mouthful that we had to eat on earth"  HAFEN & HAFEN, 158.

33    "upon this mess, we four lived for two days"  HAFEN & HAFEN, 158.

33    "have to lie flat down, at times, to keep from being swept off"  HAFEN & HAFEN, 157.

33    "point of rocks"  Edward Kern, letter to an unknown person, April 30, 1858.

35    "cold and exhaustion, [or] some other illness"  PREUSS, 147.

35    "We passed and repassed his lifeless body, not daring to stop long enough in this intense cold to perform the useless rites of burial."  HAFEN & HAFEN, 157.

35    "finish transporting the baggage to the river, to store it there in the lodge, and then to follow us"  PREUSS, 148.

35    "Taking just enough provision before it was all exhausted to do them down the river"  HAFEN & HAFEN, 159.

36    "apprehensive . . . [that] King's party [might have been] attacked!"  PREUSS, 148.

36-  "It was at this stage of things that we lost King. . . . We went on
37   a short distance and there started a fire. But King did not come."
     Thomas Breckenridge as quoted in Will C. Ferril, "The Sole
     Survivor," *Rocky Mountain News*, August 30, 1891 (BRECKEN-
     RIDGE).

37   "It was with a kind of nervous despair I raised my rifle . . . and
     we were saved"   BRECKENRIDGE.

37   "At that time . . . we seemed hardly like human beings, we were
     so near dead from hunger, cold and exposure. When I killed that
     deer we were so near starved that we ate both entrails and flesh."
     BRECKENRIDGE.

37   "the most miserable objects I have ever seen"   HAFEN & HAFEN,
     205.

39   "devouring dried deer meat"   PREUSS, 149. However, Eberhardt
     states that this should be *roasted* deer meat.

39   "hasten on down as speedily as possible to the Mouth of Rabbit
     River"   HAFEN & HAFEN, 159.

40   "In going down the other side it took us 16 days to go as many
     miles."   HAFEN & HAFEN, 138.

40   "old Elk camp"   HAFEN & HAFEN, 130.

40   "lay down upon the ice on the river and died"   HAFEN & HAFEN,
     160.

41   "near where we first struck"   HAFEN & HAFEN, 130.

41   "man left in charge was totally unfit, on account of want of tact
     and experience and correct principles"   HAFEN & HAFEN, 130.

41   leaving "the rest of us to perish"   HAFEN & HAFEN, 130.

42   "rascality almost without parallel"   HAFEN & HAFEN, 131.

42   "too weak to move"   HAFEN & HAFEN, 131.

43 "After finding that we cannot possibly bear up longer, there will then be time enough to think of adopting so horrible alternative." HAFEN & HAFEN, 164-65.

43 "Hush! said one, and we all listened intently." HAFEN & HAFEN, 165.

46 "hungry brothers" PREUSS, 151.

47 "plenty [of] big timber" HAFEN & HAFEN, 132.

47 "poor as Job" PREUSS, 153.

51 "a sled came to grief" PREUSS, 147.

# SELECTIVE BIBLIOGRAPHY

## Published Sources

GOVERNMENT DOCUMENTS

Abert, J. W. *Journal of Lieutenant J. W. Abert, from Bent's Fort to St. Louis, in 1845.* Sen. Exec. Doc. 438, 29th Cong., 1st sess., Serial 477. Washington, D.C.: Government Printing Office, [1845].

Beckwith, Lieut. E. G. "Report of Explorations for a Route for the Pacific Railroad, by Capt. J. W. Gunnison . . . near the 38th and 39th Parallels . . . " *Reports of Explorations and Surveys . . .* Vol. 2. Washington: Beverley Tucker, 1855.

Frémont, John Charles. "Abstract of Expenses and Supporting Vouchers, Third Expedition." Settlement 7634, March 9, 1849, Consolidated Files, General Accounting Office, Washington, D.C.

_____. *Geographical Memoir upon Upper California in Illustration of His Map of Oregon and California.* Sen. Misc. Doc. 148, 30th Cong., 1st sess. Washington, D.C.: Wendell & Van Benthysen, 1848.

_____. "Letter to the Editors of the *National Intelligencer* concerning the Central Railroad Route to the Pacific." House Misc. Doc. 8, 33d Cong., 2d sess., December 27, 1854, and Sen. Misc. Doc. 67, 33d Cong., 1st sess., June 15, 1854.

_____. "A Report on an Exploration of the Country Lying between the Missouri River and the Rocky Mountains." Sen. Doc. 243, 27th Cong., 3d sess. Washington, D.C., 1843.

Hayden, Ferdinand Vandeveer. *U. S. Geological and Geographical Survey of the Territories.* Washington, D.C.: Government Printing Office, 1875.

Marvin, Charles F. *Climatic Summary of the U.S.--Western Colorado.* Washington, D.C.: Government Printing Office, 1933.

*Message of the President of the U.S. Communicating the Proceedings of the Court Martial of Lt. Col. Frémont.* Sen. Exec. Doc. 33, 30th Cong., 1st sess. Washington, D.C.: Government Printing Office, 1848.

*Reports of Explorations and Surveys to Ascertain the Most Practicable and Economical Route for a Railroad from the Mississippi River to the Pacific Ocean. Made under Direction of Secretary of War, 1853-60.* 13 vols. Washington, D.C.: AOP Nicholson, 1855-60.

*Report of Explorations and Surveys from the Mississippi River to the Pacific Ocean, 1853-54.* Sen. Exec. Doc. 78, 33d Cong., 2d sess. Washington, D.C.: Beverly Tucker, 1855.

Simpson, J. H. *Coronado's March in Search of the "Seven Cities of Cibola" and Discussion of Their Probable Location.* Sen. Exec. Doc. 12, 31st Cong., 1st sess. Washington, D.C.: Smithsonian Institution, 1869.

_____. *Report of Exploration across the Great Basin of the Territory of Utah in 1859.* Washington, D.C.: Department of the Army, 1876.

_____. *Report and Map of the Route from Ft. Smith, Arkansas, to Santa Fe, New Mexico.* Sen. Exec. Doc. 12, 31st Cong., 1st sess.

_____. *Report to the Secretary of War.* Sen. Exec. Doc. 40, 35th Cong., 2d sess. Washington, D.C.: Government Printing Office, 1859.

BOOKS

Bancroft, Hubert Howe. *The Works of Hubert Howe Bancroft.* Vol. 25. *History of Nevada, Colorado, and Wyoming, 1540-1888.* San Francisco: The History Co., 1890.

Barry, Louise. *The Beginning of the West: Annals of the Kansas Gateway to the American West, 1540-1854.* Topeka, Kans.: State Historical Society, 1972.

Benton, Thomas Hart. *Thirty Years' View.* 2 vols. New York: n.p., 1850.

Bigelow, John. *Memoir of the Life and Public Services of John Charles Frémont. . .* New York: Derby & Jackson, 1856.

Brandon, William E. *The Men and the Mountain: Frémont's Fourth Expedition.* New York: William Morrow & Co., 1955.

Carvalho, Solomon Nunes. *Incidents of Travel and Adventure in the Far West. . .* New York: Derby & Jackson, 1857; Philadelphia: Jewish Publication Society of America, 1954.

Chittenden, Hiram Martin. *The American Fur Trade of the Far West.* 3 vols. New York: Francis P. Harper, 1902.

*The Daring Adventures of Kit Carson and Frémont.* New York: Hurst & Co., 1885; Worthington Co., 1887.

Dellenbaugh, Frederick S. *Frémont and '49.* New York: G. P. Putnam's Sons, 1914.

Favour, Alpheus H. *Old Bill Williams, Mountain Man.* Norman: University of Oklahoma Press, 1936.

Frémont, Jessie B. *Far-West Sketches.* Boston: D. Lothrop, 1890.

Frémont, John Charles. *The Daring Adventures of Kit Carson.* New York: James Lovell, 1885.

_____. *Memoirs of My Life. . .* Chicago: Belford, Clark & Co., 1887.

_____. *Narratives of Exploration and Adventure.* Edited by Allan Nevins. New York: Longmans, Green & Co., 1956.

_____. *Notes of Travel in California.* New York: D. Appleton & Co., 1849.

_____. *Report of the Exploring Expedition to the Rocky Mountains in the Year 1842--and Oregon and North California in the Years 1843-44.* Washington: Gale & Seaton, 1845.

Grant, Blanche C. *When Old Trails Were New: The Story of Taos.* New York: Press of the Pioneers, 1934.

Hafen, LeRoy R., and Ann W. Hafen, eds. *Frémont's Fourth Expedi-*

*tion: A Documentary Account of the Disaster of 1848-49.* The Far West and the Rockies Historical Series, 1820-1875. Glendale, Calif.: Arthur H. Clark Co., 1960.

Hart, Stephen Harding, and Archer Butler Hulbert, eds. *Zebulon Pike's Arkansaw Journal.* Stewart Commission of Colorado College and the Denver Public Library, 1932.

Heap, Gwinn Harris. *Central Route to the Pacific. . .* Vol 7. The Far West and the Rockies Historical Series, 1820-1875. Edited by LeRoy R. and Ann W. Hafen. Glendale, Calif.: Arthur H. Clark Co., 1957.

Hine, Robert V. *Edward Kern and American Expansion.* New Haven, Conn.: Yale University Press, 1962. Reprinted as *In the Shadow of Frémont: Edward Kern and the Art of Exploration, 1845-1860.* Norman: University of Oklahoma Press, 1982.

Jackson, Donald, ed. *The Journals of Zebulon Montgomery Pike with Letters and Related Documents.* 2 vols. Norman: University of Oklahoma Press, 1966.

Jackson, Donald, and Mary Lee Spence, eds. *The Expeditions of John Charles Frémont.* Vols. 1 and 2 with supplement. Urbana: University of Illinois Press, 1970-73.

James, H. L., ed. *Guidebook of the San Luis Basin, Colorado.* New Mexico Geological Society, Twenty-second Field Conference, 1971.

Lecompte, Janet. *Pueblo, Hardscrabble, Greenhorn: The Upper Arkansas, 1832-1856.* Norman: University of Oklahoma Press, 1978.

McNitt, Frank. *Navajo Expedition: Journal of . . . James H. Simpson.* Norman: University of Oklahoma Press, 1964.

Nevins, Allan. *Frémont: Pathmarker of the West.* New York: Longmans, Green & Co., 1955.

_____. *Frémont: The West's Greatest Adventurer.* 2 vols. New York: Harper, 1928.

Parkhill, Forbes. *The Blazed Trail of Antoine Leroux.* Los Angeles, Calif.: Westernlore Press, 1965.

Preuss, Charles. *Exploring with Frémont.* Translated and edited by Erwin G. and Elisabeth K. Gudde. Norman: University of Oklahoma Press, 1958.

Rittenhouse, Jack D. *The Santa Fe Trail: A Historical Bibliography.* Albuquerque: University of New Mexico Press, 1971.

Ruxton, George Frederick Augustus. *Adventures in Mexico and the Rocky Mountains.* Glorieta, N. M.: Rio Grande Press, 1973.

_____. *Life in the Far West.* Glorieta, N. M.: Rio Grande Press, 1972.

Spence, Mary Lee, ed. *The Expeditions of John Charles Frémont.* Vol. 3. Urbana and Chicago: University of Illinois Press, 1984.

Swadesh, Frances Leon. *Los Primeros Pobladores: Hispanic Americans of the Ute Frontier.* Notre Dame, Ind.: University of Notre Dame Press, 1974.

Talbot, Theodore. *The Journals of Theodore Talbot, 1843 and 1849-52...* Edited by Charles H. Carey. Portland, Oreg.: Metropolitan Press, 1931.

Thomas, Alfred Barnaby, trans. and ed. *Forgotten Frontiers: A Study of the Spanish Indian Policy of Don Juan Bautista de Anza, Governor of New Mexico, 1777-1787.* Norman: University of Oklahoma Press, 1932.

*Transactions of the Kansas State Historical Society, 1905-1906.* Edited by George W. Martin. Vol. 9. Topeka: State Printing Office, 1906.

Upham, Charles Wentworth. *Life, Explorations and Public Services of John Charles Frémont.* Boston: Ticknor & Fields, 1856.

Weber, David J. *Richard H. Kern: Expeditionary Artist in the Far*

*Southwest, 1848-1853.* Albuquerque: Published for the Amon Carter Museum by the University of New Mexico Press, 1985.

*Western Journal of Agriculture, Manufactures, Mechanic Arts, Internal Improvement, Commerce, and General Literature.* Vol. 1. St. Louis: Charles & Hammond, 1848.

White, Frank. *La Garita.* La Jara, Colo.: Cooper Press, 1971.


ARTICLES

Carter, Harvey L. "The Divergent Paths of Frémont's 'Three Marshalls.'" *New Mexico Historical Review* (January 1973): 5-25.

Ferril, Will C. "The Sole Survivor." *Rocky Mountain News,* August 30, 1891, p. 20.

Frémont, F. P. "Résumé of the Fourth Expedition." *Cosmopolitan* (October 1886). R. W. Settle Collection, William Jewell College, Liberty, Missouri.

Gwyther, George. "A Frontier Post and Country." *Overland Monthly* 5 (December 1870): 520.

"John C. Frémont." *Liberty* (Missouri) *Tribune,* July 11, 1862. R. W. Settle Collection, William Jewell College, Liberty, Missouri.

McGehee, Micajah. "Rough Times in Rough Places." *Century Magazine* (March 1891).

Miner, H. Craig. "John C. Frémont and the Southwest Pacific Railroad." *Kansas Quarterly* (Summer 1970): 40-45.

"Opening a Land of Destiny." Part 1. *Life* (April 6, 1959), 94-104.

"The Origin of Frémont's Explorations." *Century Magazine,* n.d. R. W. Settle Collection, William Jewell College, Liberty, Missouri.

Richmond, Patricia J. "An Expedition of Exploration and Survey with Lieut. William L. Marshall, U.S. Corps of Engineers, 1875." *San Luis Valley Historian* 1, No. 4 (1969): 13-18.

_____. "La Loma de San Jose." *San Luis Valley Historian* 5, Nos. 2-4 (1973); 6, Nos. 1 and 2 (1974).

*San Luis Valley Historian.* Vols. 1-6 (1969-74) and 8, No. 4 (1976). Alamosa, Colo: San Luis Valley Historical Society.

Scullin, George. "Death on the Fourth." *True,* n.d. R. W. Settle Collection, William Jewell College, Liberty, Missouri.

Settle, R. W., and Mary Lund. "The Bullheaded Pathfinder of the Rockies." *Pioneer West* (March 1968). R. W. Settle Collection, William Jewell College, Liberty, Missouri.

Simpson, J. H. "Letter Dated December 20, 1853." *National Intelligencer,* January 24, 1854.

Spencer, Frank C. "The Scene of Frémont's Disaster in the San Juan Mountains, 1848." *The Colorado Magazine* 6 (July 1929):141-46.

Voelker, Frederic E. "William Sherley (Old Bill) Williams." In *The Mountain Men and the Fur Trade of the Far West.* Vol. 8. Edited by LeRoy R. Hafen. Glendale, Calif.: Arthur H. Clark Co., 1971.

Wheelock, Walt. "Following Fremont's Fifth Expedition." Reprint from the Los Angeles Corral of the Westerners *Brand Book,* vol. 12 (1966).

MAPS

*Cities, Towns and Villages, Supplementary General Highway Map, Taos County, New Mexico.* New Mexico State Highway Department, January 1967.

Ebert, Frederick J. *Map of Colorado Territory Embracing the Central Gold Region,* 1866.

Ericson, E. S. Sketch of Frémont camps, sent to R. W. Settle, August 9, 1937. R. W. Settle Collection, William Jewell College, Liberty, Missouri.

Kern, Richard H. *Map of the Territory of New Mexico.* Santa Fe, 1851.

*A Map of Part of the Continent of North America.* Signature unclear, no date. Colorado Historical Society Collection, Stephen H. Hart Library, Denver, Colorado.

*Map of Public Surveys in Colorado Territory.* U.S. Department of the Interior, 1848 and 1866.

*Map 3 from the Santa Fe Crossing to the Coochetopa, Made under Supervision of Capt. E. C. Beckwith, 1855.* In *Pacific Railroad Surveys.* Washington, D.C.

Miera y Pacheco, Don Bernardo. *Map of . . . New Mexico.* Santa Fe, 1779. In Herbert Eugene Bolton, *Pageant in the Wilderness.* Salt Lake City: Utah State Historical Society, 1951.

*Nell's Topographical and Township Map of the State of Colorado.* Washington, D.C., 1885.

*New Sectional Map of Colorado.* In *Crofutt's Grip-Sack Guide of Colorado.* Omaha: Overland Publishing Co., 1885.

Preuss, Charles. *Map of Oregon and Upper California from the Surveys of John Charles Frémont and Other Authorities, 1848.* In *The Expeditions of John Charles Frémont.* Map portfolio. Edited by Donald Jackson. Urbana: University of Illinois Press, 1970.

Ruffner, Lieut. E. H. *Map Showing the Lines of Communication between Southern Colorado and Northern New Mexico.* Department of the Missouri, January 1, 1876.

San Isabel National Forest maps. U. S. Department of Agriculture: 1916, 1924, 1930.

Scott, Glenn R. *Historic Trail Maps of the Pueblo Quadrangle, Colorado.* Reston, Va.: U.S. Geological Survey, 1975.

Settle, R. W. Sketch of Christmas Camp location, n.d. R. W. Settle Collection, William Jewell College, Liberty, Missouri.

Siebenthal, C. E. *Topographical Map of the San Luis Valley, Colorado.* U.S. Geological Survey, 1906.

Spencer, Frank. Sketch of Frémont camps, sent to R. W. Settle, August 2, 1937. R. W. Settle Collection, William Jewell College, Liberty, Missouri.

*State of Colorado.* General Land Office, 1879.

*Thayer's Map of Colorado.* Denver: Richardson Co., 1873.

*Thayer's New Map of the State of Colorado.* Denver: H. L. Thayer, 1877.

U.S. Forest Service maps for Carson, Gunnison, Rio Grande, and San Isabel national forests. U.S. Department of Agriculture, Rocky Mountain Region, Denver, Colorado.

Van Arsdale, Perry C. *The Great Pioneer State of Colorado.* 1972.

## Unpublished Sources

DOCUMENTS

Bashford and Wagner. "The Man Unafraid." Typed copy. R. W. Settle Collection, William Jewell College, Liberty, Missouri.

Colorado Writers' Project File. Stephen H. Hart Library, Colorado Historical Society, Denver, Colorado.

Del Norte File. Kings Daughters Library, Del Norte, Colorado.

Fort Sutter Papers. Huntington Library, San Marino, California. Relevant documents include: John Chapman, "Letter Concerning Ben Kern's Property," MS 127; John Greiner, "Letter to R. H. Kern," MS 129; "Journal of Lieutenant J. H. Simpson, Santa Fe, July 23, 1849," MS 126; Edward Kern, "Memoranda Dated July 23, 1849," Vol. 31, No. 126; Richard Kern, "Report Concerning Railroad Routes to California," MS 154; Antoine Leroux, "Letter Concerning the 'Cochitohe,'" MS 130; Micajah McGehee, "Letter to Father introducing Edward and Richard Kern," MS 124; and R. S. Wootton, "Letter concerning Frémont's Route," MS 130. Western Americana Microfilm Collection, Adams State College, Alamosa, Colorado.

"Frémont's Fourth Expedition." Rio Grande County Bulletin (unpublished bulletin), County Superintendent of Schools Office, Del Norte, Colorado (five installments; 32 pages).

Gunnison, Hugh. "Captain John W. Gunnison: A Different Story." Unpublished paper, Colorado State College, Greeley, Colorado, 1962.

Kern, Benjamin. Diary of Benjamin J. Kern with the Frémont Expedition of 1848-49. Huntington Library, San Marino, California. Photostat. Colorado Historical Society.

Kern, Edward. Diary of the Fourth Expedition, 1848. Huntington Library, San Marino, California.

Kern, Richard. Diary of Richard Kern with the Frémont Expedition of 1848-49. Huntington Library, San Marino, California. Photostat. Colorado Historical Society.

Lantis, David William. "The San Luis Valley, Colorado: Sequent Rural Occupance in an Intermontane Basin." Unpublished Ph.D. dissertation, Ohio State University, 1950.

McGehee, Micajah. Typescript diary [1848-49]. Vol. 2. James Stewart McGehee Collection, Louisiana and Lower Mississippi Valley Collections, LSU Libraries, Lousiana State University.

San Miguel County, Colorado: Grantee, Grantor, School and Tax Records. Telluride, Colorado, 1878-1896.

Settle, R. W. "Frémont's Fourth Expedition." Unpublished manuscript. R. W. Settle Collection, William Jewell College, Liberty, Missouri.

"Webb Papers," Ledger 27, Day Book, pp. 10-12. Cash Book 1. *Account Books, 1848-1850.* Western Americana Microfilm Collection, Adams State College, Alamosa, Colorado.

CORRESPONDENCE

Brandon, William, to Ambrose Burkhart. Altadena, California: August 12, 1951, and March 19, 1952. Frémont file, U.S. Forest Service,

Rio Grande National Forest, Monte Vista, Colorado.

Burkhart, Ambrose, to William Brandon. Deadwood, South Dakota: March 26, 1952. Frémont file, U.S. Forest Service, Rio Grande National Forest, Monte Vista, Colorado.

Burkhart, Ambrose, to forest supervisor (memorandum). Monte Vista, Colorado: September 12, 1950. Frémont file, U.S. Forest Service, Rio Grande National Forest, Monte Vista, Colorado.

Ericson, E. S., to forest supervisor (memoranda). Monte Vista, Colorado: March 30, 1932; South Fork, Colorado: May 2, 1937. Frémont file, U.S. Forest Service, Rio Grande National Forest, Monte Vista, Colorado.

Finley, Robert B., Jr., Denver Wildlife Research Center, to Susan Collins, Laboratory of Public Archaeology, Fort Collins, Colorado: January 15, 1982. Frémont file, U.S. Forest Service, Rio Grande National Forest, Monte Vista, Colorado.

Frémont, John C., to W. B. Brown, March 9, 1848. R. W. Settle Collection, William Jewell College, Liberty, Missouri.

Hafen, LeRoy R., to A. F. Hoffman. Denver, Colorado: September 5, 1936. Frémont file, U.S. Forest Service, Rio Grande National Forest, Monte Vista, Colorado.

Hume, Joe Hyatt, to R. W. Settle. Slater, Missouri: October 3, 1937. R. W. Settle Collection, William Jewell College, Liberty, Missouri.

Kern, Edward, to Antoine Robidoux. Taos, New Mexico: February 11, 1849. Photocopy. R. W. Settle Collection, William Jewell College, Liberty, Missouri.

Kern, Edward, to unknown person, April 30, 1858 (handwritten copy). R. W. Settle Collection, William Jewell College, Liberty, Missouri.

McDaniel, Jessie Frémont Van Pelt, to R. W. Settle. Oronville, Washington: November 3, 1937. R. W. Settle Collection, William Jewell College, Liberty, Missouri.

Osherbald, Nelse F., to R. W. Settle. Kansas City, Missouri: October 3, 1937. R. W. Settle Collection, William Jewell College, Liberty, Missouri.

Ratliff, Mark, to William Brandon. Del Norte, Colorado: April 28, 1952. Frémont file, U.S. Forest Service, Rio Grande National Forest, Monte Vista, Colorado.

Reynolds, W. W., to Sterling Price, August 6, 1848. Old Files Section, Executive Division, Adjutant General's Office, War Department, Washington, D. C.

Settle, R. W., to Joe Hyatt Hume. Lamar, Colorado: October 5, 1937. R. W. Settle Collection, William Jewell College, Liberty, Missouri.

_____., to Clyde D. Sargent. Lamar, Colorado: October 5, 1937. R. W. Settle Collection, William Jewell College, Liberty, Missouri.

_____., to Frederic Voelker. Lamar, Colorado: May 26, 1939. R. W. Settle Collection, William Jewell College, Liberty, Missouri.

Voelker, Frederic, to E. S. Erickson. St. Louis, Missouri: July 9, 1942. R. W. Settle Collection, William Jewell College, Liberty, Missouri.

_____., to R. W. Settle. San Marino, California: May 23, 1939. R. W. Settle Collection, William Jewell College, Liberty, Missouri.


INTERVIEWS

Blumenschein, Helen Greene. Taos, New Mexico, December 26, 1984, and Crestone, Colorado, August 3, 1986.

Burroughs, Richard. Alamosa, Colorado, June 3-10 and June 17, 1983.

Eberhardt, Werner. Crestone, Colorado, July 30, 1987.

Elliot, Charles. Monte Vista, Colorado, September 12, 1980, and Wannamaker Creek, La Garita Mountains, Colorado, September 28, 1980.

Keck, Charles. Del Norte, Colorado. February 20, 1990.

Mrs. Millyar, History and General Department, St. Louis Downtown Public Library. July 1980.

Neamon, Mary. Monte Vista, Colorado, October 6, 1981, and August 28, 1986.

Ward, George. Saguache, Colorado, September 2, 1975, and October 5, 1980.

Wilkinson, Ernest. Monte Vista, Colorado, October 4. 1980.

White, Frank. Capulin, Colorado, September 11, 1980.

attempting winter expedition, 58-59; argues with Williams over route, 11, 13, 73; sends out relief party, 23; leaves Vinsonhaler in charge of main group, 30; initiates second relief party, 35; knowledge of San Luis Valley settlements, 82; encounters first relief party, 37, 38; trades supplies for assistance, 81; in Taos with Kit Carson, 46; departs Taos for California, ix, 47; reasons for leaving Kerns in Taos, 84-90; blames disaster on guide Williams, 84; dislike of Ben Kern, 88; praised for leadership during ordeal, 90; possible lost diary of, xviii
Frémont's fourth expedition. *See* Fourth expedition
Frémont relief party, 30, 35, 38-39. *See also* King relief party; San Juan, Chief

Garcia (Colo.), 47,
Gardner Butte, 7, 61
Geban Creek, 16, 72, 74; origin of name, 17, 78
Geyer, Charles, vi
Godey, Alexis, xix, 30, 46, 53, 54, 74, 89 (*in chronological order*): supports Williams's Carnero route, 12-13, 84; accompanies King relief party, 24; returns from King relief party, 26, 28; on Frémont relief party, 35; relief mission of, 22, 39, 40, 42, 43-44; rescues Manuel, 40; encounters stragglers, 43; discovers bodies of victims, 44; abandons effort to retrieve cache, 44. *See also* Frémont relief party
Grape Creek, 64
Great Sand Dunes, 8, 63-64; crossed by fourth expedition, 9; modern travel over, 9; origin of, 63; and prehistoric sites, 63
Great Sand Dunes National Monument, 8, 63-64
Greenhorn Peak, 61
Greenhorn Trail, 61
Gregorio, 53; leaves Kern party, 41-42
Groundhog Creek, 16, 19, 31, 72, 74, 77
Groundhog Creek camp, 29, 87; location of, 31
Gunnison, John W., 56, 62; camps near Great Sand Dunes in 1853, 9;

describes Carnero Pass, 68; describes San Luis Valley, xvii; expedition of, 9, 10, 55; murder of, 55

Halfmoon Pass, 23
Hardscrabble (Colo.), 61; founded, 4; mountain men at, 4-5
Hardscrabble Canyon, 6
Hardscrabble (White Oak) Creek, 6
Head, Lafayette, 70
Heap, Gwinn Harris, 45, 62, 66, 67, 85
Hell Gate, 13, 70; origin of name, 71
Hibbs, Al, 77
Hubbard, George, 30, 54; death of, 44; quoted, 6
Huerfano Butte, 61
Huerfano River, 6, 7, 61, 62
Huerfano Valley, 61
Hume, Joe, 80

Indians at Big Timbers, 1-2
Inscription Rock, 17-18; location of, 73

Joaquin's Trail, 70
Johns Creek, 16
Juan, 53; leaves Kern party, 41-42

Kearny, Stephen Watts, viii, 2, 3
Keck, Carl, 51; discovers artifacts, 27
Keck, Charles, 27
Kern, Benjamin, 2, 17, 33, 78, 90; dislike of Frémont, 88; ill, 24-25, 28; left in Taos by Frémont, 47; murdered by Utes, 54; sketches Hardscrabble Canyon, 6; quoted, 6-7, 10-11, 14, 19, 20, 26, 29-30. *See also* Kern brothers
Kern, Edward, 30, 53, 73, 84, 91; blames Frémont for Proue's death, 88; criticism of Frémont, 87, 90; feels betrayed by Frémont, 87, 90; left in Taos by Frémont, 47; quoted, 2; retrieves Ben Kern's body, 54. *See also* Kern brothers
Kern, Mary, 87, 89
Kern, Richard, 7, 16, 19, 20, 23, 32, 47, 54, 61, 91; almost lost on return trip, 47; denounces Vinsonhaler, 41, 42; "hermit's camp" of, 29-30; left in Taos by Frémont, 47; murder of, on Gunnison expedition, 55; quoted, 24, 28, 32, 40-43, 46, 89; reason for joining fourth expedition, viii; sketches and watercolors:

of Cave Creek, 14
of East Embargo Creek, 28-30
"Point of Rocks," 34
"Proulx Creek," 71
"The Relief Camp," 45, 83
"Robidoux' Pass," 6
of sand hills, in 1853, 9
of Sierra Blanca, 45
of Spanish Peaks, 62
Kern brothers, 78, 91; accused of
 cannibalism, 88-89; antagonize other
 members, 87-88; diaries of, 55;
 reluctance of, to do menial labor, 87;
 suffer depression, 29, 30
King, Henry, 8, 53, 86; death of, 36-37;
 leads first relief party, 23-24; possible
 lost diary of, xviii. *See also* King relief
 party
King relief party, 23-24, 37-39. *See also*
 Frémont relief party

La Garita (Colo.), originally named
 Carnero, 13
La Garita caldera, 70, 72
La Garita camp (Vinsonhaler's), 29, 33;
 location of, 31-32
La Garita Creek, 13, 15, 29, 33-34, 45,
 71; canyon of, 33; flood pattern of, 69;
 as route of descent from Mesa
 Mountain, 26, 40
La Garita Mountains, 1, 14-15, 25, 74
La Garita sheepherders, 17, 71, 73-74;
 accompany Godey, 22
Lake Fork, 11
La Loma del Norte, 67, 70
Lama (N. Mex.), 50
La Placita (N. Mex.), 92
La Sauses (Colo.), 45-46, 48
La Sauses Gorge, 39
Las Palomas (Taos), 92
Lawrence, John, 69, 70
LeBlanc, Antonio, 83
LeBlanc, Jose de La Luz, 83-84
LeBlanc, William, 47, 83
LeBlanc family, treasure tales of, 78
Leroux, Antoine, 70; as guide for
 Gunnison expedition, 10; helps
 retrieve Ben Kern's body, 54;
 knowledge of Cochetopa country, xvi;
 wagon road of, 67
Leroux Creek (Rito Alto), 10, 66
Loma (Colo.), competition of, with Del
 Norte, 80-81

Longe, 5, 54
Luders Canyon, 11

McDowell, James, 54
McGehee, Micajah, 1, 26, 42-43, 54; dis-
 courages cannibalism, 43, 89; quoted,
 2-3, 5, 8, 13, 19, 25, 29, 32-33, 35, 36,
 40, 43
McNabb, Theodore, 35, 54
Manassa (Colo.), 48, 91
Manuel, 44, 46, 53; rescued, 40
Martin, Thomas, 18, 26, 31, 40, 41, 43,
 46, 53, 82, 88; argues for split in
 party, 42, 45; reminiscences of, 56
Martinez, Antonio Jose, 92
Maxwell, Lucien, 4; on Frémont's first
 expedition, vii
Médano Creek, 8
Médano Pass (Williams's Pass), 8, 9, 61,
 63; origin of name, 64; modern travel
 over, 64
Mesa Mountain, 11-12, 16, 31, 71, 74,
 78, 86; avalanche dangers on, 18;
 geography of, 72; mistaken as
 Continental Divide, 15
Miera y Pacheco, Don Bernardo, map
 of, 40
Mill Creek, 68
Miners Creek, 15
Moffat (Colo.), 12, 66
Monte Vista (Colo.), 36, 38
Moon Pass, 11, 85
Mora (N. Mex.), 54
Morin, Antoine, 53; death of, 42
Mormons, at El Pueblo, 3, 60
Mosca (Colo.), 61
Mosca Creek, 8
Mosca Pass, 7-8, 9, 61; origin of name,
 62-63

New Year's Eve camp, 28
North Pass, 11

Palmer Mesa, 22-23, 86; possible
 intended route of Bill Williams, 20
Perry Creek, 16, 71, 74
Pfeiffer, Albert, Jr.: discovers Frémont
 artifacts, xiv, 24-25; discovers Frémont
 camps, 76; visits site of "Camp
 Dismal" in 1928, 22
Pike, Zebulon Montgomery, expedition
 of, 8, 9, 45, 53, 58, 59, 63, 66, 69
Pike's Stockade, rendezvous site, 38-40

Pinos Creek, 34
Point of Rocks, 44; described by
Edward Kern, 78; identified, 33-34;
location of, 34-35; drawn by Richard
Kern, 34
Poso Creek, 14, 71
Preuss, Charles, 18, 20, 23-25, 30, 41,
43, 46, 47, 53, 55, 64, 86; 1848 map of,
xvi; on Frémont's first expedition, vii;
leads group to Palmer Mesa, 20; maps
of, and their importance, vii; on
Frémont relief party, 35; praises
Frémont's leadership, 90; questions
Williams's route to San Luis Valley, 8;
quoted, 20, 35, 36, 51; steps of,
retraced by author, 85; supports
Williams's Carnero route, 12-13, 16,
84. See also Frémont relief party
Promontory Divide, 6, 64
Proue, Ralph, 30, 53, 88; death of, 35;
creek named after, 71
Pueblo (Colo.), 54, 61, 92

Questa (N. Mex.), 39, 49-50, 81

Rabbit River. See Conejos River
Railroads: search for route through
Rockies, 68; surveys of, and Civil
War, 56-57, 86
Ramon, Agua, 23
Ratliff, Mark, 25, 77
Red River, 50, 81
Red Wing (Colo.), 7
Rincon Creek, 19, 23, 26, 27, 36, 38;
initial descent on, 25
Rincones (Colo.), 82
Rio Colorado villages, 24, 46-47
Rio Grande, 9, 45, 63, 66, 85, 92;
changes in course of, 45, 69; early
explorations of, 91; tributaries of, 72
Rio Grande Canal, 12, 45
Rio Grande Gorge, 91, 92
Rio Grande del Norte. See Saguache
River
Rio Grande Valley, 66
Rio de Tres Tétones. See Crestone
Creek
Robidoux, Antoine, 84; wagon road of,
xvi, 7, 8.
Robidoux Pass. See Mosca Pass
Rohrer, Henry, 42, 54; death of, 43, 89-
90

Romero, Epimenio, discovers sledges in
1930, 77
Rudolph Mountain, 6
Ruxton, George Frederick, 3, 50, 60

Saguache (Colo.), 69
Saguache Canyon, 66
Saguache River, 66; changes in course
of, 12, 69; Frémont's goal in crossing
sand dunes, 9; in Miera y Pacheco
map, xv; mistaken for Colorado River,
19; as "Rio Grande del Norte," xv,
xvii
Sagauche Valley, 11, 85; snowfall in, 75
San Acacio (Colo.), 48, 49, 91
San Antonio River, 82
San Cristobal (N. Mex.), 50, 81
Sand hills. See Great Sand Dunes
San Fernando (N. Mex.), 92
San Francisco (Colo.), first settlement on
Conejos River, 82
San Francisco Creek, 34
San Gabriel (N. Mex.), 64
Sangre de Cristo Mountains, 6, 7, 14,
15, 56, 62, 64, 92
Sangre de Cristo Pass, 61
San Juan, Chief, assists Frémont, 81
San Juan Mountains, 5, 9, 10, 25, 56, 57,
66, 80-81; average snowfall in, 58;
geology of, 33
San Luis (Colo.), 48, 49, 70
San Luis Creek, 9
San Luis Hills, 37, 38, 91; site of
reunion with Godey, 45
San Luis River, 66
San Luis Valley, 9, 13-14, 56, 59, 64, 69,
91, 92; average snowfall in, 58; early
settlements in, 48-49, 82-84, 70, 81;
first seen by fourth expedition, 7-8;
geography of, xiii-xiv; lack of
firewood in, 66; lithographs of, in
Gunnison report, 55; Mormons in, 3;
mosquitoes in, 62; routes leading to
west from, 68; severe weather conditions of, 17, 41, 47, 53; Spanish names
for geographical features in, 63; trails
of, 11, 39, 48-49, 70; wetlands in, 10-
11. See also Rio Colorado villages
San Margarita (Colo.), 82
San Pedro Mesa, 49
Santa Fe (N. Mex.), 59, 60, 92
Saunders, Jackson, 54; on Frémont relief
party, 35